dumb (dum) *adj.* Ignorant or stupid. Lacking sense.
dumber (dummer) *adj.* See above. Only more so.
dumbest (dummest) *adj.* See below.

- The convicted rapist who sued prison officials because his cookie fell apart
- The USDA officials who suggested that pig privates be dyed green to discourage people from snacking on them
- The teenager who burned down his house to kill a really big, hairy spider
- The husband who shot his wife because he mistook her for a rat
- The merry widow who was fined for dancing on her late husband's grave while singing "Who's Sorry Now?"

And other 100% factual, 100% bizarre examples of behavioral buffoonery too outlandish not to be true. Here are the world's greatest lamebrains, nitwits, morons, and fools living life to their jawdropping dumbest.

John J. Kohut is a political analyst for a large corporation in Washington, D.C. He has been collecting strange news clippings for more than a decade and is the author of *Stupid Government Tricks*. **Roland Sweet** is a magazine editor and writes his own syndicated column. Kohut and Sweet co-authored *Dumb, Dumber, Dumbest* and *News From the Fringe*.

MORE
DUMB,
DUMBER,
DUMBEST

True News of the
World's Least
Competent People

Compiled by John J. Kohut
and Roland Sweet

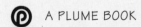 A PLUME BOOK

PLUME
Published by the Penguin Group
Penguin Putnam Inc., 375 Hudson Street,
New York, New York 10014, U.S.A.
Penguin Books Ltd, 27 Wrights Lane,
London W8 5TZ, England
Penguin Books Australia Ltd, Ringwood,
Victoria, Australia
Penguin Books Canada Ltd, 10 Alcorn Avenue,
Toronto, Ontario, Canada M4V 3B2
Penguin Books (N.Z.) Ltd, 182–190 Wairau Road,
Auckland 10, New Zealand

Penguin Books Ltd, Registered Offices:
Harmondsworth, Middlesex, England

Published by Plume, an imprint of Dutton Signet,
a member of Penguin Putnam Inc.

First Printing, January, 1998
10 9 8 7 6 5 4 3 2 1

Ⓟ REGISTERED TRADEMARK—MARCA REGISTRADA

Library of Congress Cataloguing-in-Publication Data
Kohut, John J.
More dumb, dumber, dumbest : true news of the world's least
competent people / compiled by John J. Kohut and Roland Sweet.
p.   cm.
T.p. verso.
ISBN 0-452-27891-0
1. Curiosities and wonders—Humor.   I. Sweet, Roland.   II. Title.
PN6231.C85D86   1998
081—dc21   97-34063
CIP

Printed in the United States of America
Set in Century Book
Designed by Jesse Cohen

For Bob Rickard and Paul Sieveking

Introduction

Since the publication of our previous compilation, *Dumb, Dumber, Dumbest*, we have noticed a spate of books in the same vein. What surprises us most about these other collections, however, is the infrequency of duplication. Clearly, the lack of common sense is more widespread than even we had assumed.

Confirming that observation is this sequel. It yields more than 500 all-new, all-true examples of human ineptitude. As exhaustive as our efforts to chronicle human folly have been, we can read only so many newspapers a day. If you would care to amplify our quest, please contribute original clippings or photo-copies (no Internet postings, please), citing date and source, to:

Strange News
P.O. Box 25682
Washington, D.C. 20007

Meanwhile, enjoy these further dispatches from a strange planet.

1.
DUMB
HAPPENS

Dumb As I Wanna Be

After Robert Ricketts, nineteen, was hit in the head by a train in Bowling Green, Ohio, he explained to police that he was trying to see how close to the moving train he could place his head without being hit.

Fumble

Boston Patriots defensive end Bruce Walker suffered a stab wound in his chest that required five stitches to close while he and a friend were playing catch with a steak knife outside a Super Stop & Shop in North Attleboro, Massachusetts, and Walker missed.

Cyberspace Cadet

Judith Kraines, county controller of Reading, Pennsylvania, complained at a county commissioners' meeting that she had to use a typewriter because her computer was old and no one had been able to get it to work for two years. Three days later she announced that she had discovered what was wrong with her computer and now it was working fine. It had not been plugged in.

RESCUE ME

• In Winona, Minnesota, Mary Tyler, thirty-nine, had to summon firefighters to rescue her after she got her hand stuck in the toilet trying to retrieve her deodorant, which had fallen in.

• After picking up a distress signal, Britain's Royal Air Force assembled an air-sea rescue team that spent three hours looking for the source of the emergency signal. Finally the RAF helicopter landed at a truck stop, where the crew found the distress beacon in a truck. It was on its way to be repaired when a bump in the road apparently triggered it.

• Norwegian scientists tracking the migratory routes of wild salmon were excited to pick up a radio signal from one fish they had given up for lost. They followed the signal to the city of Stavanger, where they found it—and the fish—in a fisherman's freezer.

WHEN ASPIRIN ISN'T ENOUGH

Police in Chieti, Italy, freed a girl who had been locked in a dark room for more than six years because she had a headache. Carmela Borchetti was sixteen when her uncle, a fortune teller, declared that the headache meant she was possessed by evil spirits. The only cure, he explained, was to spend seven years in a dark room, so her parents put her in her bedroom and fastened the shutters. Acting on a tip, police found Borchetti, now twenty-two, who at first insisted that she did not want to be rescued. "Go away," she told police. "I must lie here for six more months, and then I can live again."

CURB YOUR APPLIANCE

In Christchurch, New Zealand, a woman answered loud knocking at her door at 5:15 A.M. to find a man holding a color television set. He said he was having difficulty finding his way out of her property. She gave him directions, then checked to make sure the TV wasn't hers. Ten minutes later police called to an unrelated matter at a neighbor's place found the man, still carrying the TV. He satisfied officers that it belonged to him but couldn't explain why he was wandering around in the dark with it, according to a Sergeant Kortegast, who commented, "It has left us wondering if there are not enough dogs to go around."

CHOKING RICH

Adam Kane Morris, twenty-three, of Kew, Australia, choked to death on a wad of ten fifty-dollar bills that investigators concluded he had swallowed during a fit in the bath. Nine days later in Buffalo, New York, a robbery suspect who tried to swallow incriminating evidence choked to death on a fifty-dollar bill.

LITTLE BANG THEORIES

• Phil Cram, forty-two, police chief of Medway, Maine, out fishing with two companions, tried to put a homemade bomb in the water to stun fish so he could scoop them up when they floated to the surface. The device exploded prematurely, blowing off his hand from the thumb down.

• In Medina, Ohio, a construction worker brought a homemade three-and-one-half-foot-long double-barreled cannon to work. Coworkers expressed curiosity about how much noise it could make, so the worker loaded it with black gunpowder and fired it. According to police Lieutenant Dave Snows, the explosion caused a piece of the cannon to fly off a considerable distance and hit construction worker Richard M. Houdek, thirty-one, in the head, killing him.

• Bonnie Booth, thirty-eight, was hospitalized in Muncie, Indiana, after shooting herself in the foot while using a shotgun to try to remove a callus. "She told investigators she drank a gallon of vodka and two or three beers and tried to shoot the callus off her foot," police Captain Baird Davis said. "She told officers she had already tried to cut off the callus with a razor, and it didn't work. She was afraid it was getting infected because it hurt real bad."

• At an American Legion club bar in Watford City, North Dakota, rancher Robert Mead, Jr., complained about the quality of the beer he was served and left. According to witnesses, he returned with a lever-action rifle in one hand and a semiautomatic rifle in the other. Customer Patrick Wagner reported, "He fired a shot into the ceiling and then said, 'Now, bring me a real beer.'" Police were called, and when Officer Keith Braddock arrived, Mead fatally shot him and took two other men hostage for nine hours before walking out at 2:20 A.M.

• Police in Andover, New Jersey, reported that a husband and wife, he forty-seven years old, she thirty-eight, were slightly injured when they lit a stick of dynamite inside their car and went to toss it out only to realize then that they had forgotten to roll down a window.

• In Fairfax County, Virginia, Ian Priestland, twenty-nine, was making an explosive device as an experiment, using a piece of pipe cut from a bicycle frame. He decided the best way to crimp and cap off the end of the pipe was to hold it and hit it with a sledgehammer. When he did, the device blew up in his hand.

Out of Focus

Several hours after a fatal three-car accident on the Massachusetts Turnpike, Peter Nicholas, sixty-one, sold exclusive photographs of the crash scene to a newspaper in Framingham. Later state police charged Nicholas with running over one of the two victims, then leaving the scene after he stopped to photograph the accident. Bill Thompson of the *Middlesex News*, who bought the pictures from Nicholas, said, "This kind of thing gives photographers a bad name."

Oops!

• In El Cajon, California, Heather Jaehn, twenty-five, and her boyfriend returned home but discovered they had misplaced the house key. When they couldn't find an open window, the hundred-pound Jaehn decided to try the chimney. Partway down she got stuck. Her boyfriend tried unsuccessfully for three hours to get her out before calling the fire department. Meanwhile Jaehn had removed a sweater she was wearing because it was getting too warm in the chimney. When finally rescued, she was covered with soot and "naked from the waist up," according to fire department Battalion Chief Ed Jarrell. Pointing out that she was greeted by thirteen firefighters and an assortment of television cameras and still photographers, he added, "She was pretty embarrassed about the whole thing."

• In Carbondale, Illinois, Jon Podbielski and Bob Czernik chained themselves to a locked gate at 5:00 A.M. to protest construction of an incinerator at the Crab Orchard National Wildlife Refuge. Unfortunately for them, refuge officials said, the blocked gate wasn't the entrance to the incinerator construction site but to a wastewater treatment plant on the refuge. As a result, U.S. Fish and Wildlife officials didn't become aware of the two protesters until that afternoon. Then, because Podbielski and Czernik had squirted superglue into the U-shaped bicycle locks they had chained themselves with so the keys wouldn't work, rescue workers ended up cutting through a brace on the gate to free the men, leaving the locks around their necks.

• Timothy O'Brien killed himself after thinking he had missed out on winning $3.2 million in Britain's National Lottery when he and his gambling partner forgot to place their weekly wager and their regular number came up. Coroner Roy Barter explained that O'Brien had indeed won but misread the numbers and actually would have gotten only $43.

• In Japan, Teruo Mochizuki, a right-wing activist upset over the government's proposed bailout of failed housing lenders, decided to make his opposition known by smashing his car into the Finance Ministry's offices. He apparently misread the street map, however, and ended up two blocks away, his car stuck in a steel barrier outside the National Police Agency, where he was arrested.

• A Boeing 757 flown by Aeroperu Airlines crashed into the Pacific Ocean in 1996, killing all seventy people on board. The cause of the crash was determined to be pieces of duct tape placed over air pressure, altitude, and airspeed sensors by workers who were polishing the outside of the airliner. They forgot to remove the tape when they were finished.

IN THE DRIVER'S SEAT

• José Pinto, who is ninety-five percent blind, drove himself to work for three years until Madrid police arrested him after receiving a tip-off from his employer, Spain's National Organization of the Blind. Records showed that even though police stopped him just the year before for not having a license, they never noticed his poor eyesight. Pinto explained he found his way through seven miles of city streets each day by avoiding shapes and shadows. Arresting officers reported his car had no dents or scratches.

• Wendy Maines was driving through Versailles, New York, when she saw five dogs attacking a cat. She stopped to rescue the cat, scaring off the dogs by honking her horn and slamming the door. Figuring the cat had run into the woods, she started to drive off but felt a bump. It was the cat, now flat, she admitted, adding, "Maybe it was just Mother Nature's way of telling me to mind my own business."

THE NAME GAME

• A district court in southern Sweden fined Elisabeth Hallin $680 for naming her five-year-old son "Brfxxccxxmnpcccclllmmnprxvclmnckssqlbb11116." She said the name is pronounced "Albin." The Hallins said they would appeal the fine, arguing that the name is "a pregnant, expressionistic development that we see as an artistic creation."

• Constance Miller, sixty, told a state trooper that she killed her eighty-three-year-old mother in the mobile home they shared in Union City, Pennsylvania, because she grew tired of her mother calling her by her middle name. "She said that she didn't like being called Agnes," trooper Dana Anderson testified. "She wanted to be called Connie."

• A Michigan judge denied John Jakubowski's request to change his name to "Kiss My Ass," despite Jakubowski's insistence that the change was a protest against years of conflicts over local laws, property rights, and property taxes. The judge said that he believed Jakubowski would "hide behind the name as a way to use the expression," suggesting a scenario of what would ensue if he was stopped by a police officer while driving.

SEX IS ITS OWN PUNISHMENT

• In Prince William County, Virginia, a couple who had just finished watching an X-rated video at the twenty-three-year-old woman's house decided to act out a fantasy involving a naked hitchhiker. After dropping her off, the thirty-five-year-old man was supposed to circle the block and pick her up, according to police spokesperson Kim Chinn. "A car began to approach her and, thinking it was him, she jumped out in the road with her thumb out. But it wasn't him." The driver sped by and stopped at a fire station a half mile away. Firefighters sent an ambulance, which gave the naked woman a hospital gown and called police. After officers arrived, finally the man showed up, only to be charged with driving under the influence.

• A Nashville, Tennessee, jury convicted Raymond Mitchell III, forty-five, of tricking women into blindfolding themselves and having sex with him by claiming to be their boyfriend. Prosecutors said most of the hundreds of women that Mitchell called hung up, but of the thirty women who reported the encounters to police, eight said they had sex with the caller. One woman admitted having sex with the man twice a week over two months until she discovered he wasn't her boyfriend during one encounter when her blindfold slipped off.

• In Denver, David Joseph Zaba, thirty-two, pleaded guilty to assault for pouring varnish on his wife during sex instead of the honey and chocolate syrup she was expecting. Angela Zaba said that the varnish made her hair fall out. The police report on the incident said the couple have been using food as part of their sex life for six or seven years, noting that the wife "stated that this is not the first time that he has used varnish, but she has had enough, so she called police."

• Israel Zinhanga, twenty-eight, told a Zimbabwe court that he had sex with a cow because he was afraid of contracting AIDS from a human partner.

• After picking up money from a bank in Dayton, Ohio, Wells Fargo armored car driver Aaron McKie decided to engage the services of a prostitute. They had sex in the vehicle, FBI Agent Peter A. Lakes noted, adding that after the "female exited the armored van, McKie no-

ticed that the bag with the bank's $80,000 was missing."
When McKie reported the incident, he lost his job.

Odd Ends

• Michael P. Olson, thirteen, was found dead in Eau
Claire, Wisconsin, with his entire head wrapped in duct
tape and a roll of duct tape next to the body. Police, who
concluded that the tape suffocated the boy, discovered
another roll and wads of tape in his bedroom. Michael's
sister, Errin Olson, nineteen, told police her brother was
"simply obsessed with any kind of tape."

• In England, Mark Gleeson, twenty-six, suffocated
in his sleep after stuffing two tampons up his nose to
stop his snoring.

• Police in Santa Rosa, California, reported that
Gary Bowers had been bothered by woodpeckers and
tried using a pellet gun to drive them away. Unsuccess-
ful, he bought a shotgun. The first time he went to use
it, he slipped on his front porch on the way to his targets, and the gun fired, killing him.

• Williamsport, Pennsylvania, authorities who found
the body of would-be burglar Henry Carlton, forty-one,
wedged halfway through a basement window concluded
that he froze to death because the two sweatshirts and
bulky coat that he was wearing to keep warm stopped
him from squeezing through the fifteen-by-eighteen-inch

window. "Now he's wedged in there, he's on his stomach, the more he struggles, the more his clothing bunches up against him, his feet are off the ground, and he can't get any leverage," Lycoming County Coroner George Gedon explained, concluding that Carlton passed out from the pressure on his chest and abdomen, then froze.

FAMILY MATTERS

Robert Barzyk was sentenced to thirty days in jail for oinking at his ex-wife whenever he saw her walk past his house in Penbrook, Pennsylvania. Rachel Nickle, who lives several houses from her ex-husband, said he made pig and elephant noises for nine years. Deputy District Attorney Diana Woodside added that last year he began supplementing the animal sounds by playing "Old MacDonald" on a cassette player.

JUDGE NOT LEST YE BE JUDGED

In Dadeville, Alabama, three men holding a contest to determine their knowledge of the Bible each quoted different versions of the same passage. One of the men checked his Bible and realized he was wrong, then shot and killed the man who beat him, Gabel Taylor, thirty-eight. Police Chief Terry Wright quoted witnesses as saying the suspect "said Taylor did know more and that made him mad."

MAN'S BEST FRIEND

Authorities in Hillsborough County, Florida, accused Robert Meier, fifty-five, of marrying his forty-nine-year-old girlfriend Constance Sewell just hours before her death as she lay in a coma, then running up nearly twenty thousand dollars on her credit cards. Detective Ed Hancock said Meier admitted that what he did was wrong but explained "he was sitting on the couch when Sewell's dog told him she would want him to go on living, have a better life and it would be OK to use her credit cards."

IT'S ALL CNN'S FAULT

Los Angeles sheriff's deputies arrested Hugo Hernandez, twenty-two, as one of two men suspected of shooting out the windows of more than 250 motorists. One deputy testified that Hernandez said that the acts gave him an "ultimate rush, referred to himself as the 'O. G. [original gangster] freeway vandal' and asked if I'd seen him on TV."

WHEN YOU GOT IT, FLAUNT IT

During a hearing to consider lawyer F. Lee Bailey's request that the government pay him $1.4 million to cover his costs for representing a major drug dealer, the prosecutors suggested instead that Bailey owed the government $412,322. They questioned his charges, including reimbursement for meals costing $655, trips to resorts in Switzerland and France, $550-a-night hotel rooms in Europe, and the filet mignon and 200 roses he sent to a prison inmate. The last item was part of a total of $103,689 that was to go to Bailey's bookkeeper for running errands for the drug dealer while he was incarcerated, including bringing him sushi.

ONE MORE REASON NEVER TO DO THIS

A man in West Plains, Missouri, set himself on fire in a suicide attempt, then had second thoughts and leaped into a pond to put out the flames. He drowned.

DUDE, COME QUICK!

A thirty-year-old Maryland man called 911 to report a fire on his property. "You gotta put out the fire, man," he told the dispatcher. "My marijuana plants are burning." When firefighters arrived, they found the man sitting in the dark in the kitchen strumming a guitar. At his sentencing he admitted to the judge, "I made some stupid mistakes."

WOULDN'T KNOW SPIT FROM SHINOLA

When police in Stamford, Connecticut, discovered a rubber fetus in a road, they mistook the medical training device for the real thing and called in an assistant medical examiner. The assistant medical examiner also mistook it for the real thing and sent it away to be autopsied.

THE RICH ARE DIFFERENT FROM YOU AND ME

According to a former confidant of convicted murderer John du Pont, the millionaire once attended a South American wrestling tournament masquerading as a Bulgarian because he was afraid of being kidnapped. Because he couldn't speak Bulgarian, he also had to pass himself off as mute.

IT'S A RODENT'S LIFE

Robert Dorton greeted authorities investigating complaints that he was keeping rats in his motel room in Billings, Montana, by opening fire on them. Police and fire crews needed tear gas and a water cannon to subdue the man, who was seen kissing one of the rats and referred to them as "my brothers."

SOME PEOPLE

After opening a Ku Klux Klan museum and apparel store, called The Redneck Shop, in Laurens, South Carolina, John Howard told a reporter that he had encountered little objection. "The only people I've had a problem with, who took it as an insult and a racial situation, have been blacks," he explained. "I didn't know blacks here were so prejudiced."

GOOD NEWS, BAD NEWS

• After waiting two years for a heart transplant, Ralph Bregos, forty, received news at his Kentucky home that a donor had been found. According to authorities, he became so excited that he had a heart attack and died.

• While workers installed plumbing and a bathroom in her three-room cabin in Bath County, Virginia, to supply running water for the first time in her life, Margaret Mae Bee, ninety-six, moved into a nearby motel. Although she usually used only a washcloth to clean herself and apparently had never bathed in a tub, she decided to take a bath. She filled the tub with water, but, according to the state medical examiner's office, it was so hot that she died from the scalding. "She forgot to put the cold water in," said a relative, Barbara Wright.

SHOW-OFF
Navy investigators determined that Lieutenant Commander John Bates, thirty-three, crashed his fighter jet into a Nashville, Tennessee, house, killing himself and four other people, while attempting a "maximum performance" takeoff into thick cloud cover without permission. Rear Admiral Bernard Smith, commander of the Center for Naval Tactical Warfare, said he believed Bates attempted the risky maneuver to impress his parents, who were watching from the ground.

STRANGE REACTIONS
After commuter train crew members in Darien, Connecticut, suspected they had run over a body, they made an emergency stop and found a naked man lying in the space between the tracks. He was not only alive but also angry, according to Metro-North police officer James Pymm, who explained, "When the workers turned their flashlights on, he jumped up and started beating them."

GUNPLAY

• Police in Sandusky, Ohio, charged Lowell Altvater, eighty, with negligent assault for firing a shotgun at what he said he thought was a rat in his barn. It actually was his wife's hat, which she was wearing. Three years earlier Altvater had fired at what he thought was a rat in the barn, but it turned out to be his own leg.

• In Lancaster, South Carolina, Richard Gardner, twenty-three, was nailing some molding at his mother-in-law's house but didn't have a hammer, so he used a .25-caliber handgun that he thought was empty. He shot himself in the hand and his wife in the stomach.

• Domenico Germano, thirty-two, was sentenced to four years' probation and ordered to pay $5,433.09 to repair an automated teller machine in Portland, Maine. He admitted firing four shots at the ATM when it balked at his repeated attempts to withdraw cash with his bank card.

• Brandon T. Lally, twenty-three, of Reston, Virginia, was preparing to leave a party to play basketball, but his sister didn't want him to take his 9 mm semi-automatic pistol with him. To show her that it was safe, Lally removed the magazine, placed the gun to his head, and pulled the trigger. The gun fired, killing Lally.

BIRDBRAIN

When sanitation workers in Uniondale, New York, arrived at the home of Roderick Baker, seventy, to clean up his garbage-filled yard, he tried to keep them from removing the twenty tons of debris by holding 140 chickens hostage at knife point, threatening to kill 1 chicken a minute until the sanitation crew left his property. He had killed 3 of the birds before authorities intervened.

CURSE OF THE DRINKING CLASS

After Felix Rivera found his neighborhood Pik Nik convenience store closed for the night, the San Antonio, Texas, resident greased up his body with used cooking oil from a vat behind the store and slid in through a roof vent. Even so, he got stuck, with his legs dangling from the store's ceiling. His break-in set off the store's burglar alarm. Eight firefighters took an hour to pull him up through the vent. Store manager Joe Castellano, who had been called to the scene, said Rivera "walked up to me and said, 'Sorry, man. All I wanted was a beer.' Because of the alarm, he was pretty deaf after he left."

DRUMMING UP BUSINESS

• New York State Police in Buffalo arrested James Isaac Mitchell, twenty-two, after investigators concluded the volunteer firefighter set fires at two vacant houses, a hunt club, and a rural church, then returned with his fire company to fight the blazes.

• Authorities accused Joy Glassman, sixty, of setting five fires in the Shasta Trinity National Forest to help her son, a seasonal firefighter with the U.S. Forest Service. "She wanted him to be able to go and fight a lot of fires and make extra money," said Mark Reina, an investigator for the California Forestry Department. Each fire was extinguished before a half acre had burned.

• Baltimore police robbery detective Arnold Adams was accused of calling in tips on his own cases to Metro Crime Stoppers, which offers rewards of up to two thousand dollars for tips that lead to arrests. The *Baltimore Sun* reported that the twenty-eight-year veteran had friends collect the rewards.

DOESN'T ADD UP

After Rutgers University math professor Walter Petryshyn, sixty-seven, was charged with beating his wife to death with a hammer, longtime friend Bohdan Boychuk said Petryshyn may have been driven insane by a math error he made. After Petryshyn published the textbook *Generalized Topological Degree and Semilinear Equations*, Boychuk "noted very drastic changes" in his friend, he said. "He discovered that there was some mistake in that book and he told me that mistake was very serious, very big and he couldn't solve it."

Actually, Petryshyn's publisher, Cambridge University Press, considered the error a minor omission and said the book was well received and selling well. His editor, Lauren Cowles, had dismissed the mistake as "a technicality" and had dealt with it by sending corrections to reviewers for academic journals.

OPTIONAL EQUIPMENT

Redondo Beach, California, police officer Joseph Fonteno stopped a car after observing it heading along the Pacific Coast Highway with half of a traffic light pole on its hood and the signal lights still attached. Fonteno said that when he asked about the pole, the driver explained, "It came with the car when I bought it."

MENSA REJECTS

• Don Ramirez, sixteen, told police in Canberra, Australia, that after seeing a movie in which James Bond uses a spray can as a makeshift flamethrower, he tried to kill a spider by setting bug spray on fire. The resulting explosion started a blaze that burned down his family's house and scorched a car parked outside.

• Jeffrey Pollen was hospitalized with burns covering most of his upper body when his wood pellet stove exploded. Authorities in Prince William County, Virginia, said Pollen had used gunpowder to try to get the fire going.

MISSED BY A MILE

After Phuoc Bui, thirty-four, was fired from a Packard Bell computer plant in Sacramento, California, for "distributing literature to other employees about taking up arms against supervisors," he returned to the plant with a 9 mm semiautomatic pistol and fired forty rounds before a security guard wounded him. Police spokesperson Michael Heenan reported the only person injured was Bui.

JUSTICE SERVED

Renato Salazar entered his company's kitchen in Manila and opened two cooking gas tanks. Hiding inside a water-filled drum to protect himself, he tossed a lighted match at the tanks, starting a fire that destroyed the building. Despite Salazar's foresight, the heat from the blaze boiled the water in the drum, killing him.

REASONABLE EXPLANATION

Police investigating the stabbing of Melvin Moses, thirty-six, in Desmet, Idaho, said that his wife, Brenda, told them she was only trying to give him a tonsillectomy when she shoved a seven-inch butcher's knife down his throat.

CHEW ON THIS

Authorities in Kanawha County, West Virginia, concluded that Mark A. Howell, thirty-one, died while driving his pickup truck when he opened the door to spit out tobacco juice and struck his face on a rock.

NUCLEAR FAMILIES

Emergency officials in Ukraine said a fire that engulfed five deserted villages near the Chernobyl nuclear power plant may have been caused by a burning cigarette discarded by picnicking families visiting graves near their former homes.

NONFATAL ATTRACTION

When their parents disapproved of their relationship, Huang Pin-jen, twenty-seven, and Chang Shu-mei, twenty-six, attempted suicide by driving a car off a cliff in central Taiwan. Huang was seriously injured, and Chang suffered minor injuries. A month later, according to police in Kao-hsiung, they tried to hang themselves in their hotel room with bedsheets. When that failed, the couple held hands and jumped from the twelfth floor of their hotel. They landed on the roof of an adjacent five-story restaurant and were hospitalized with bone fractures. "We notified their parents, and

they didn't seem surprised at the renewed suicide bid,"
police officer Chang Fang said. "But they agreed to settle their dispute with the young couple."

SPELLING COUNTS

Dan O'Connor, twenty-two, filed a suit against a tattoo
parlor in Carlstadt, New Jersey, for misspelling the
"Fighting Irish" slogan he paid $125 to have tattooed on
his arm. The inscription reads, "Fighing Irish." "I can't
just live with this," O'Connor said. "You're not talking
about a dented car where you can get another one.
You're talking about flesh."

LIAR, LIAR, PANTS ON FIRE

In Bridgeport, Connecticut, police called to the scene
of a shooting found Kevin Hall, eighteen, lying on the
ground, clutching his groin. His pants, which had a
large hole, were still smoking. He explained he was the
victim of a drive-by shooting, but his girlfriend said
Hall had bragged about having a sawed-off shotgun in
his pants. When he tried to pull it out to show it to her,
it fired, blasting his genitals. To add insult to injury, police charged Hall with possession of the weapon.

AVIATION FOLLIES

After Royal Jordanian Airlines received a call that a passenger on an Amsterdam to Chicago flight was carrying a bomb, the jet was diverted to Iceland, where 224 passengers were forced to wait fifteen hours at the Reykjavik airport. Officials traced the call to a Chicago woman, who, airline spokesperson Monib Tukaan said, "didn't want her mother-in-law to come to Chicago. She admitted having made the call and said she didn't think anyone would believe her."

THE DEVIL MADE ME CHEW IT

Pittsburgh-area waitresses Sybil M. Peck, thirty, and Julie L. Kelley, twenty-nine, filed a federal lawsuit against a restaurant they said fired them after they complained about a satanic ritual involving a Barbie doll that was skewered, broiled, and deep-fried. The women said some managers and workers routinely talked about "worshiping the devil" and played "blaring and repetitious music in the kitchen" regarding the "sacrificing and desecration of humans."

SPIRITED DRIVING

Maryland police reported that after James D. Padgette, Jr., thirty-five, turned in to a parking lot to make a

U-turn, his door came open, and he fell out, then was run over by his car. He wasn't seriously hurt but reportedly tried to drive away in a car that looked like his but wasn't. The owner called police, who charged Padgette with driving while intoxicated.

First Things First

An ambulance in Hampshire, England, transporting heart attack victim Peter Jones, forty-one, to a hospital four miles away, took forty minutes to complete the trip because the first crew's shift ended, and the driver stopped at the ambulance station to change crews. "The second crew realized I was having a heart attack, and I had a needle stuck in my arm right away," said Jones, who spent a week in the hospital.

Quest for Fat

Fearing that an ammonia leak at a Dreyer's ice cream plant in Union City, California, might have affected the taste of its ice cream, company officials tried to bury six hundred thousand gallons of it without any publicity. Word got out, however, and officials reported a mob of people descended on the ranch where the ice cream was being buried to grab a few gallons before it melted. Dreyer's asked the ranch owners to stop the people, but the owners also had to turn away about ninety trucks that had been hauling in the ice cream. After Dreyer's had already covered about two acres with six million dollars' worth of ice cream, Stanislaus County officials informed the company that although burying contaminated ice cream isn't illegal, burying the paper and plastic containers it comes in is.

DASHED HOPES

In Florida, Steve Trotter was forced to postpone his attempt to leap from St. Petersburg's sixty-story Sunshine Skyway Bridge two weeks before the scheduled stunt when he fell out of a tree and broke his neck.

STUPID IS AS STUPID DOES

• Authorities investigating the deaths of Marlin Ray Baker, twenty-five, and his girlfriend, Carolyn Boyd, thirty-one, speculated that Baker had seen a certain phone number repeatedly on Boyd's Caller ID and assumed that a lover had called, so he beat her to death. He subsequently killed himself after discovering that it was just a repeated wrong number.

• David Keeton died near Tustin, California, after his car plunged down an embankment. Witnesses said Keeton had been swerving all over the road to keep the car behind him from passing.

RIDING THE RAILS

Mike Wright, seventeen, jumped aboard a train outside Crofton, Kentucky, hoping for a quick ride into town. By the time his journey ended, he had traveled two thousand miles. The train did not stop in Crofton but continued on to Evansville, Indiana, sixty-five miles to the north. Wright switched trains and, believing he was on his way back home, fell asleep. He awoke to find someone had closed and latched the door to the insulated produce car. A week later two railroad workers in Hermiston, Oregon, discovered Wright when they heard him calling for help.

AMAZING FEAT

After winning a seat in the Philippine Congress, former first lady Imelda Marcos reported that thanks to the kindness of friends and supporters, she has been able to replenish the thousands of shoes confiscated when she and her husband fled the country, claiming, "I have more shoes now than before."

NEXT TIME, WEAR A DISGUISE

Michael Coulter, thirty-two, was arrested in Ireland for shoplifting after clerks told police to be on the lookout for a man who was so tall that he had trouble entering the shop. At seven feet five inches Coulter holds the distinction of being Ireland's tallest man. The previous year Coulter had been scheduled to launch a nonsmoking campaign in Ulster schools, but he was dropped after being convicted for stealing cigarettes from a gas station in Lifford.

LIVING WELL IS THE BEST REVENGE

André-François Raffray was forty-seven when he proposed paying ninety-year-old Jeanne Calment $500 a month until she died, at which time he would move into her grand apartment in Arles, France. Raffray's deal seemed like a bargain, but thirty years later he died at age seventy-seven, having paid $184,000 to Calment, who at age one hundred and twenty was declared the world's oldest living person. Although Raffray already paid more than twice the apartment's current market value, his agreement obligates his widow to keep sending a monthly check as long as Calment lives.

CARRY-ON BAGS MUST FIT IN THE OVERHEAD COMPARTMENT

Two men and a woman kidnapped Jason Stanley, twenty-one, of Gravette, Arkansas, tied him up with plastic handcuffs and duct tape, then locked him in a soft-sided zippered suitcase, which they kept in their backseat for four days while driving through Missouri,

Oklahoma, and Texas. At one stop a four-year-old girl claimed she heard a voice coming from the suitcase until the abductors convinced her luggage couldn't talk. Finally Stanley talked them into releasing him, sore and bruised but otherwise unharmed. "He's about six foot," Benton County sheriff's investigator Sergeant Sam Blankenship pointed out, "but he's got a slender build."

GIVE PEACE A CHANCE

The California Highway Patrol reported that a driver pulled up beside a slower-moving pickup truck in Orange County and repeatedly tried to strike it with a baseball bat. After missing and denting her own car with the bat, she crossed the yellow double line and threw a can of air freshener at the truck as she passed. After the confrontation Officer Peros Doumas chased down the woman, Lisa Lind, twenty-six, who told him "she was in a hurry and getting frustrated." Then Doumas noticed the woman's license plate: PEACE 95. "She told me she got it because she thought there was so much violence going on in today's society," he said.

UNHOLY PANIC

• In Kansas City, William H. Irvin III was entitled to a government check for $183.69 but because of a computer error received $836,939.19. He spent more than $300,000 before authorities caught up with him and charged him with misconduct. Irvin's defense was that he believed the money was a gift from God because it appeared after he had visited a lonely road one night and prayed for a means of self-sufficiency. "If you believe in God, you believe in miracles," Irvin's attorney, Willard Bunch, told the jury. "He prayed for it, and he got it." Skeptical jurors convicted him.

• Nancy Bell, forty-six, had applied to join the Zion Lutheran Church in East Moline, Illinois, and was serving a probationary period while members evaluated her when she accidentally crashed her car into the church one morning just after one o'clock and was arrested on DUI charges.

BACK TO THE DRAWING BOARD
In Lancashire, England, Ian Lewis, forty-three, spent thirty years tracing his family tree back to the seventeenth century, traveling all over England and interviewing two thousand relatives, before he learned that he had been adopted when he was a month old and that his real name was David Thornton. He said he would immediately start researching his new family history.

HIGH JINKS

Cheap poison used by the New York City health department to control rats is instead causing them to become "psychotic," according to workers in the Bronx, who complained that the drugged rodents were strolling into offices in broad daylight. Health department spokesperson Sam Friedman denied that the city's extermination efforts were making the rats crazy, but workers also complained that they were finding dead rats in their desk drawers and filing cabinets.

LOVE HURTS

In Bountiful, Utah, Bruce Jensen, thirty-nine, discovered that his wife of three and one-half years was a man. The deception by Felix Urioste, thirty-four, unraveled when Jensen filed a missing person report and police learned that Las Vegas, Nevada, authorities had arrested Urioste for using fraudulent credit cards issued to Bruce and Leasa Jensen to run up at least forty thousand dollars in debt. He was traveling as a bearded man.

Authorities said the feminine-looking Urioste, who had already had his testicles, but not his penis, removed in anticipation of a sex change operation when he met Jensen at the University of Utah Health Sciences Center while masquerading as a female doctor, never let Jensen see him naked during their celibate marriage. Jensen wed Urioste out of a sense of obligation after Urioste claimed to be pregnant with twins after their lone sexual encounter. Urioste later said the twins were stillborn. "I feel pretty stupid," Jensen said, adding that he wanted an annulment, citing irreconcilable differences.

DESIGNATED DRIVER

Police in Fort Lauderdale, Florida, said Sandra D'Avanzo, thirty-seven, didn't trust herself to drive home after having drinks at dinner, so she told her ten-year-old daughter to take the wheel of the Mercedes-Benz. The child made it as far as three doors from home when she ran off the road and crashed into a neighbor's front yard.

FOLLOW THE LEADER

• Six people drowned while trying to rescue a chicken that fell down a sixty-foot well in the Egyptian village of Nazlat Imara. Police said an eighteen-year-old farmer, his sister, two brothers, and two elderly farmers who came to help climbed down one by one, but all drowned, apparently after being pulled down in the water by an undercurrent.

• Five fruit processors perished picking pickled mangoes from a storage tank in Udon Thani, Thailand. They had hooked up a radio to listen to while they worked, but the extension cord dropped into the tank. Police said the first worker died trying to retrieve the cord. The rest died one by one trying to rescue the others.

PEOPLE, GET IT STRAIGHT!

An explosion at a home for the developmentally disabled in Santa Ana, California, raised part of the roof, dislocated two walls, and shattered windows. Estimating damage to the four-bedroom house at $125,000, investigators blamed the blast on fifty bug bombs that detonated near a gas stove pilot light, according to Santa Ana fire department spokesperson Karl Feierabend, who observed, "They were fumigating for bugs and kind of overdid it."

NEARER MY GOD TO THEE

After an argument Nigel David, twenty-eight, left his girlfriend's home in Syracuse, New York, to look for a place to pray. He told police he scaled an eight-foot fence around an electric company substation and climbed a fifteen-foot transformer tower. As he grabbed for a wire to lift himself, 34,500 volts of electricity hit him, burning a third of his body. David's accident didn't surprise his twenty-eight-year-old girlfriend, who told police he sometimes climbs trees and utility towers.

JUNK MAIL JUNKIE

Police in Roanoke, Virginia, accused Ann Kennedy Dickens, sixty-two, of stealing her neighbor's mail, the third time she has faced such charges in five years. Postal Inspector Kevin Boyle said 460 pieces of mail were found, unopened, neatly stacked and boxed in her back bedroom. In 1990 Dickens was charged with stealing more than 5,000 pieces of mail. In 1993 she was charged with stealing about 450 pieces. This time she was released but on condition that she stay at her residence except on Sundays—when there is no mail delivery.

TOE THE LINE

• An immigration agent at Toronto's Pearson International Airport was suspended after he ordered people entering Canada to remove their shoes and socks. The agent, who officials acknowledged had been counseled four times for similar complaints, told visitors that official policy required them to remove their footwear so he could photograph their feet.

• Police in Cook, Australia, accused Thomas Borkman, twenty-four, of breaking into the apartment of a thirty-one-year-old woman who had never met him and supergluing his face to the sole of her foot while she slept. Emergency surgeons needed three hours to separate his face from her foot. A police official speculated that Borkman's motive "had some sexual significance."

MR. FIXIT

• Unable to find a drill to bore a hole in his car's exhaust pipe, Joseph C. Aaron, twenty, of Wesley Chapel, Florida, got his gun and tried to shoot one in it. The bullet fragmented when it hit the pipe, and pieces hit Aaron in the leg.

• In Halifax, Massachusetts, police accused Robert Brinson, twenty-eight, of trying to blow up his ex-girlfriend and her family at home using two bombs like the one that blew up the federal building in Oklahoma City. Police said Brinson's bombs were considerably less dangerous because he mistakenly used potting soil instead of fertilizer.

DO AS I SAY, NOT AS I DO

• When Miguel Gonzalez, thirty-one, reported for his anger management class in Honolulu drunk and disruptive, police said anger counselor Charles Mahuka, thirty-nine, lost his temper and beat Gonzalez into a coma.

• After just eight days on the job Boston's new transportation commissioner William E. Luster, thirty-six, was fired amid revelations that he had twice parked illegally in Boston, including blocking a handicap ramp while in town for his job interview. The car was ticketed and towed. In addition, the man in charge of traffic safety and parking already had at least five speeding tickets and three accidents on his record, as well as two arrests for driving with a suspended license between 1989 and 1994. He also had an unpaid parking ticket, which put him on the Registry of Motor Vehicles' license nonrenewable list. Luster's driving record was so poor that he had been compelled just the year before to take the remedial road safety course required of the state's worst motorists.

• Despite their denunciations of the federal government as a "corporate prostitute," Freeman Ralph Clark and his partners on the ranch that was the site of the 1996 Freeman standoff with federal law enforcement officers in Montana received $676,082 in checks from the federal government during the last decade in payments from farm subsidy programs designed to cushion such farming setbacks as droughts and low prices for products.

No Place Like Home

Unhappy with his room at a Danish center for asylum seekers, a twenty-eight-year-old Bosnian refugee was found living in the Copenhagen Zoo. Authorities said he moved into a hayloft above the antelope, where he hung pictures and lived for a month before being discovered.

A JOURNALIST TO THE END

In Belgrade, Montana, Glenn Sorlie, editor of the *High Country Independent Press*, died of a staph infection on a Tuesday. His widow waited until Thursday to report the death to authorities so that his weekly paper could publish his obituary before the *Bozeman Daily Chronicle*. She explained, "He wouldn't want to get scooped on his own death."

SALESMAN WITH A BANG

Authorities in Rogers, Arkansas, charged Johnny Lee Nichols, twenty-five, with going door to door trying to trade dynamite for sex or drugs. They found five and one-half sticks of Dyno-Omnimax in his car.

LOVE IS A LOSING THING

After Stephen Perisie hit the Ohio lottery twice, winning $3.1 million, his wife tried to hire a hit man to kill her husband to collect the $107,000 a year her husband is collecting for twenty years. Prosecutor Frances McGee said the couple's twenty-one-year-old son overheard Kim Kay Perisie discussing the idea with her boyfriend and called police. An undercover officer posed as a killer for hire, and she offered him $500, giving him a $25 down payment. Perisie said despite the affair and the murder plot, he still loves his wife and wants to patch things up. The thing that upset him the most, he said, was the low price she put on his head.

It's All Happening at the Zoo

• One man was killed and another injured at the Calcutta Zoo after they decided to enter the enclosure of a thirteen-year-old Royal Bengal tiger and put a marigold garland around its neck to celebrate New Year's Day.

• A twenty-eight-year-old San Diego man was mauled by two Manchurian brown bears after entering their enclosure at the San Diego Zoo. The man, who underwent emergency surgery for a gash to his groin, explained to police that he went in after the animals motioned for him to join them.

That May Be So, Nevertheless . . .

Police in Milford, Connecticut, stopped a fifty-year-old man for running a red light only to have him start screaming, "We're all going to hell!" as he tried to light a pipe bomb in his front seat with his cigarette. Police wrestled the bomb away from him.

PILTDOWN MAN WITH A GUN

A thirty-seven-year-old man in Getzville, New York, argued with his brother after a pizza delivery boy forgot
to bring soda with the delivery. The man did not think
the boy deserved to be paid and yelled, "He should
have brought the Pepsi!" before firing two shots at his
brother through a closed door.

NEW AGERS GONE BAD

A fully clothed woman was pulled from the Atlantic
Ocean three miles off Fort Lauderdale after a boater
saw her treading water. She explained to rescuers, including the Coast Guard, Fort Lauderdale police, and
the Broward County Sheriff's Office, that she was actually living in the sea, couldn't live on land anymore, and
did not want to be rescued. She explained that she was
"transitioning" to life in the sea and was spotted because she had "just come up to get some air."

POWER TO THE PEOPLE

Michael Marcum, twenty-one, was jailed for stealing
six four-foot-tall, 350-pound transformers that police
found at his home in Stanberry, Missouri. He explained
that he needed them to power a time machine. The
sheriff said that Marcum had hooked up one of the

transformers to the fuse box at his house and created a
"Jacob's ladder," consisting of a V-shaped antenna with
electrical sparks arcing from side to side. Four transformers were found in the living room. One had been
emptied of oil and was being used as a coin bank. The
one transformer in use was draining power from other
homes in the small town. "People's lights would go out,
or sometimes just go a little orangy," the sheriff said.
"They weren't too happy about it."

FIRST THINGS FIRST

Summoned to a burning two-story town house, two
paid and six volunteer firefighters in Prince Georges
County, Maryland, began to quarrel over who should be
first to carry the hose into the building. The argument
escalated into a fight that required county police to
break up.

MAN ON A MISSION

Early in 1996 Salim Juma Mubarak of the United Arab
Emirates attained one-third of his goal of fathering
sixty sons. The father of twenty-two sons and twenty
daughters said, "If God wills, I may get sixty sons."
Mubarak has four ex-wives, and lives with three current Indian wives and the forty-two children in one
house. At the time all three women were pregnant and

expecting within three months. Nine other children had died shortly after childbirth.

SHORTSIGHTED

Three Ethiopian hijackers, armed with an axe, a fire extinguisher, a bottle of whiskey, and something they claimed was a bomb, took over an Ethiopian airliner as it left the capital of Addis Ababa bound for Kenya. They demanded that the pilot fly to Australia, ignoring his explanation that the plane didn't have anywhere near enough fuel. Two and one-half hours later, the plane ran out of fuel and crashed into the Indian Ocean just off a resort beach near Mozambique. Two of the hijackers survived the crash, along with fifty-two other people aboard.

BRAIN FIGHT!

Four medical students at Tokyo's Kashima University were dissecting cadavers when one student pulled part of a cerebral cortex from a skull and threw it at another student. All four then began throwing brains at one another and went to the windows of the second-floor lab and started to throw brains at people walking past. The four were expelled, with one blaming the incident on the pressures of study and no sleep.

REALLY BAD HAIR DAY

Michelle Rosati, a waitress in Yardley, Pennsylvania, sued Richard ("Lefty") Clunn over an incident in which he came up behind her at the bar and used a butcher knife to cut off her ponytail. Rosati sought a thousand dollars an inch for the nineteen-inch ponytail that she had been growing for ten years. Clunn explained he had been arguing with another patron about the sharpness of the knife in question and decided to prove a point.

NEXT TIME THE DOG DRIVES

A twenty-five-year-old Maryland man was convicted of animal cruelty after neighbors turned him in for repeatedly "car-walking" his hundred-pound Chesapeake Bay retriever by driving at 30 mph while holding the dog's leash out the car window, forcing the animal to keep up. "At the time I did it, I thought it was good," the man told the court. "I thought it was healthy, good for him."

PEOPLE WHO SHOULD LIVE IN BEIRUT

The New York State Corrections Commission suspended state prison guard Glenn Goord without pay after it was pointed out that he had been flying a Nazi flag from the porch of his home. Goord told a local newspaper that he was not a racist or a Nazi but flew the red, black, and white banner simply because "I like the colors."

PEOPLE UNAWARE OF THE POTENTIAL FOR IRONY

Two robbers wound up in intensive care after trying to mug two men outside a club in St. Louis at 2:00 A.M. The cries of the victims were heard by a group of their friends and relatives inside the club who rushed out and beat the would-be thieves. It all happened outside the Stop the Violence Club.

YO! HEL-LLOOOOO!

After spending eleven years in prison for two rapes that DNA tests finally proved he did not commit, Walter Smith was released. Upon his release Smith said, "It's kind of sad because you get attached to different people in prison."

QUICK, GIVE HER SOME FRIES!

A twenty-one-year-old woman in Lebanon, Oregon, became enraged when she was mistakenly given an order of chicken rather than hamburgers at a McDonald's drive-through window. She crawled through the window and proceeded to throw food and drinks at the employees, then destroyed the cash register. When police arrived to arrest her, they found her waiting in line at the drive-through window of a nearby Taco Time restaurant.

EVERYBODY'S GOT A HOBBY

When authorities attempted to serve a Columbiana, Alabama, man with a court order, a standoff ensued. Police fired thirteen rounds of tear gas into his home before he surrendered. The man's relatives said that his years of sniffing gasoline explained his tolerance for the gas.

WHATCHA DOIN'?

The U.S. Environmental Protection Agency spent fifty thousand dollars cleaning up the backyard laboratory of an eighteen-year-old in Union Lake, Michigan, who had collected radioactive elements from old smoke detectors and lamps, constructed his own Geiger counter, and isolated gases and acids in various jars. He even had some radium. "He was trying to isolate all the elements on the periodic table," said an EPA radiation expert. During the operation an EPA team in protective suits packaged all the contents of a backyard shed into thirty-nine fifty-five-gallon drums to be shipped to a radioactive waste dump in the Utah desert.

Now You Tell Me
A Danish Maersk Airlines passenger jet en route from England to Italy had to make an emergency landing in Lyons, France, after the copilot broke into a sweat and announced to the pilot that he was afraid of heights.

Indeed, Look What Happens!
A couple living in a San Diego motel awoke one morning to find their pet nine-foot Burmese python wrapped around the wife, who was eight months pregnant, squeezing her stomach and biting her buttocks. When the husband tried to use a knife to free her, the snake entwined him too. After neighbors using a crowbar failed to get its mouth off the woman, paramedics responded and cut the snake's head off with a hacksaw. "It was more like a puppy dog than a snake," the husband said afterward. "It would follow you around the house. For some reason, it woke up and felt it needed to attack." He noted that his wife is "naturally scared of snakes, but I've been begging her for years to let me get a snake—and look what happens."

PEOPLE WHO DON'T GET CABLE

A man in Belton, Missouri, woke up his seventeen-year-old son at 6:00 A.M. on a Saturday and told him to mow the lawn. The boy said that it was too early and told his father to go away. The man returned with the mower, pushed it through the bedroom door, and started it up in the room, its blades cutting clumps from the carpeting. The boy threw a fan at the mower and called police, who arrested the father for assault.

IF ONLY LIFE WERE THIS SIMPLE

Two men in Michigan were hospitalized after a carnival game operator hit them on the head with a mallet after the two had been fighting over prizes from the Ring the Bell stand.

CAPTAIN BEEFHEART, ABOUT THIS ALBUM TITLE

People for the Ethical Treatment of Animals asked the mayor of Fishkill, New York, to change the town's name to Fishsave. *Kill* means "stream" in Dutch, the language spoken by the town's settlers.

CURLY'S PROTÉGÉ

In Owensboro, Kentucky, a Davies County road department driver attempted to drive a twenty-ton dump truck across a bridge with a posted weight limit sign of three tons. He had made it halfway across when the bridge collapsed.

IF BEAVIS AND BUTTHEAD COULD FLY A PLANE

Two pilots of an Italian fire fighting plane were under investigation after they twice "dive-bombed" bathers near the popular tourist resort of Villasimius, off Sardinia. The crew had been asked to put on a display during a pageant for the feast of Our Lady of the Shipwrecked. Police said that they got their coordinates wrong and twice dropped thousands of gallons of water on the assembled spectators, capsizing boats and injuring ten people.

HEY, YOU, GET OFF MY PLANET

Martin Juergens, fifty-nine, of Westphalia asked the German government to uphold his ownership of the moon against a 1980 claim by Rio Vista, California, entrepreneur Dennis Hope, who sold seventeen hundred lunar lots for sixteen dollars each. "The moon has belonged to my family since 15 July, 1756," said Juergens, claiming Prussian Emperor Frederick the Great gave the moon to his ancestor Aul Juergens, to thank him for a blessing that Frederick said brought him great foreign policy success, and decreed "that the moon should remain in my family's possession forever and should be passed on to the youngest-born son."

WHY CABDRIVERS REALLY DO RULE THE WORLD

After a North Korean submarine ran aground in South Korea, a massive seven-week manhunt ensued for the sub's twenty-six crew members, assumed to be spies. The last two were killed in a firefight near the border. According to diaries and photos found on their bodies, the two North Koreans had successfully eluded sixty thousand South Korean soldiers assigned to search for them and managed to photograph key military installations along their route. They also spent at least one night playing video games at a crowded ski resort. In the face of growing press criticism over the handling of the affair, the South Korean defense minister said that negligent officers would be disciplined, including the commander whose unit failed to detect the sub after it had run aground. The sub had instead been initially discovered by a cabdriver who happened to be driving by.

FAMOUS
MOUTHS

WHY DON'T YOU GO BACK TO . . .
NEVER MIND

Aleksandr Solzhenitsyn refused to vote in Russia's December 1996 parliamentary election, calling the electoral system "unjust, unfair" and one that "does not allow the people to express themselves." Said the famed dissident: "In fact, such a system gives the people nothing and can give the people nothing."

A FUTURE IN THE DIPLOMATIC CORPS

Performing during a heat wave in West Bloomfield, Michigan, Blood, Sweat and Tears lead singer David

Clayton-Thomas remarked to the crowd that it was "as hot as the last train car going to Auschwitz."

WELL, AH, WELL, THANKS MARLON . . .
I THINK

Appearing on *Larry King Live*, Marlon Brando said, "Hollywood is run by Jews. It's owned by Jews, and they should have a greater sensitivity about the issue of people who are suffering." Noting stereotypes portrayed in films over the years, Brando went on: "We've seen the . . . greaseball. We've seen the Chink. We've seen the slit-eyed dangerous Jap. We have seen the wily Filipino. We've seen everything. But we never saw the kike because they knew perfectly well that that's where you draw the wagons around." Later he added, "Thank God for the Jews. The Jews are amazing people."

PRESENTING THE MOST CEREBRAL
"WORLD CONFEDERATION OF WRESTLING
NITRO!"—ONLY ON TNT!

Speaking to an international forum of foreign journalists, media mogul Ted Turner said, "The United States has got some of the dumbest people in the world. I want you to know that, we know that. It's a disgrace." He continued, "When you've got eighty channels like you do here [in the United States], people watch whatever they want. And that's the sad thing about it, because the more cerebral, the more complex, the more forward-looking the story is here in the United States, to a large extent the smaller the ratings are."

(Bonus Turnerism: Speaking to journalists in 1995, Turner, unable to purchase a major television network, said that he "felt like the Jewish people in Germany in 1942.")

The Heartbreak of Inbreeding
With a debate on gun control raging in Britain following the slaughter of sixteen children at a school in Scotland, Prince Philip entered the discussion over banning handguns: "I mean, look, if somebody, if a cricketer, for instance, suddenly decided to go into a school and batter a lot of people to death with a cricket bat, which he could do very easily, I mean, are you going to ban cricket bats?"

And That Allusion Would Make Charlie Sheen Who?
Hollywood madam Heidi Fleiss told *Jerusalem Report* magazine: "I don't know about comparing myself to [convicted spy] Jonathan Pollard, but I certainly see myself as

a victim of police and government anti-Semitism. I suppose a better comparison would be to the Rosenbergs."

You've Come a Long Way, Baby

General Yuri Glazkov, deputy commander of Russia's Gargarin Cosmonaut Training Center, said that cosmonauts aboard the space station *Mir* were looking forward to the arrival of U.S. astronaut Shannon Lucid because "We know that women love to clean." Lucid, fifty-three, a biochemist, made four previous shuttle flights before the *Mir* mission.

2.
WHO'S IN CHARGE?

PRIORITIZATION

After laying off more than two hundred workers to help close a budget gap, the Los Angeles Metropolitan Transportation Authority announced it was spending $1.3 million to replace bus drivers' brown uniforms with blue ones. "It's a morale booster," MTA spokesperson Andrea Green said, indicating the change was an attempt "to elevate the stature of the bus operators" in neighborhoods so they'll be regarded "like police officers or firefighters."

OOPS!

• Scientists from Utah State University and Russia worked for two years, spending seven million dollars from the Defense Department, to build an antimissile satellite. A day after the 550-pound, fifty-nine-inch satellite was launched on its thirty-day mission, it failed. After a three-month investigation USU scientists concluded that the Russians had connected solar panels to recharge the satellite's battery backward. "They were hooked up in reverse polarity," USU engineer James Cantrell said, "and had the effect of discharging the battery instead of charging it."

• Workers cleaning up a school storeroom in Costa Mesa, California, mistakenly threw away some three thousand rare fossils that had just been cataloged. The collection was being stored at Lindbergh Elementary School during summer vacation in seventeen boxes, all wrapped and each marked with a list of contents on top. The Mesa Consolidated Water District, which had paid ninety thousand dollars to collect and identify the fossils, didn't discover the loss until August—too late to recover them.

• When Paul Holloway, a professor at the University of Florida, landed at Orlando after a flight from Amsterdam, he pointed out to police that one of his bags was torn. A search yielded explosives in his luggage. Upon further investigation, authorities discovered that Dutch police planted the explosives without detonators to test airport security measures, then forgot to remove them after the exercise. Dutch Justice Minister Winnie Sorgdrager admitted that police had routinely planted explosives in passengers' luggage daily for the past seven years.

• In Grottoes, Virginia, rookie police officer David E. Broad, forty, informed Chief Charles K. Lawhorne, forty-eight, that he was having problems taking his gun out of his town-issued holster. Lawhorne called Broad to his house for some training "to save your life." They practiced quick draws with unloaded weapons, and when Broad thought the session was over, he reloaded to return to duty. As he was heading out the door, the chief clapped and told him to draw just one last time. Thinking he was "still in training mode," Broad turned and pulled the trigger, shooting the chief in the chest.

GOTTA LEGISLATE

• California Senate Majority Leader Henry Mello proposed a bill that would appropriate $132,000 a year for removing tattoos from young people. An aide explained the bill was aimed especially at youths released from the California Youth Authority who emerge with tattoos in visible places—hands, face, and neck—that make finding jobs difficult. The conservative newsletter *Inside California* objected to the legislation, declaring, "Tattoos help identify criminal suspects."

• Belgian Agriculture Minister Karel Pinxten proposed legislation banning camel and ostrich racing, even though neither is known to occur anywhere in Belgium.

• During a deadlock over the legitimacy of Taiwan's new cabinet, Fu Kun-cheng, deputy whip of the opposition New party, got into an argument with Shen Chih-hui of the ruling Nationalist party over who should address Parliament first. When Shen refused to let go of a tag giving her priority over Fu, he bit her on the hand and kneed her in the thigh.

CAN'T BE TOO CAUTIOUS

Alerted to sixty-four tiny piles of white powder along a 2.2-mile stretch of streets between San Marino and Pasadena, California, authorities dispatched a hazardous materials team and warned area pet owners of a possible attempt to poison animals. After spending six hours cleaning up the still-unidentified substance, officials were informed the powder was ordinary baking flour marking a trail for a race.

PLEASE PEE HERE

An Irish intercity bus passing through Tuam, County Galway, stopped to let passengers use the public toilet. Finding the facility closed for demolition, one woman went to the rear of the building, on the bank of the Nanny River. As she stooped to go, she lost her balance and fell into the river. Two men working in the yard of a nearby hardware store heard her cries for help and rescued her. "We got her dried up as well as we could," said store worker Padraig Glynn, "and the other passengers on the bus then used our toilets."

Councillor Joe Burke said the incident highlighted the need for a public toilet in Tuam, declaring, "People passing through the town should be able to attend to their bodily functions with dignity, and they should not need to bring a change of clothes with them."

HEAD GAMES

• Concerned about the number of very short haircuts at his west London Ealing division, police Superintendent Bill Troke-Thomas warned officers who refuse to let their hair grow that they risk being assigned to desk duty. He insisted the public may regard such haircuts "as intimidating or even thuggish."

• Farther north, Manchester's seven thousand police officers began trading their high-topped constable's helmets for American-style caps, despite a protest by Brian Mackenzie, president of the Police Superintendents Association. "The helmet provides stature, height, authority, and protection." Chief Constable David Wilmot said the officers were more interested in hats that fit inside a police car and won't fall off during a foot chase. The officers also traded their belted tunics for bomber jackets.

HANDS OFFICIALLY OFF

Queensland, Australia, issued a workplace health and safety guide covering the state's growing crocodile industry. Besides advising crocodile handlers not to "place any part of one's body in the mouth of a crocodile," the guide points out the occupational hazards of collecting crocodile eggs, "show" feeding, and capturing adult crocs—especially if the boat is smaller than the reptile. Under the heading "Unsafe Activities," the guide warns: "Do not sit on the back of a crocodile."

GUILTY VICTIM

In England, Dorothy Dunn, forty-eight, was fired from her job at Greater Manchester's Tameside General Hospital for taking three months off after being told by the hospital that she had angina. The diagnosis turned out to be wrong, so the hospital ruled that her time off was inexcusable.

OVERDUE FOR SENSITIVITY TRAINING

Fort Lauderdale, Florida, police detective Don McCawley was fired after performing a skit at a "Good Ol' Boy Roundup" in which he pulled a painted black doll from a hollowed-out watermelon and began beating it. McCawley had been singled out in a Justice Department report for his performance at the annual gathering of law enforcement officials, which it said included rampant drunkenness, performances by strippers, and other misconduct.

LIKE A BAD PENNY

Most disbarred lawyers who seek readmission to the bar eventually are allowed to practice again, even though many may have to reapply four or five times, according to the *National Law Journal*. "With little fanfare and some downright secrecy," the *Journal* reported, lawyers disbarred for bank robbery, estate fraud, witness tampering, even abetting murder "are welcomed back into the bar."

IF YOU CAN'T SAY SOMETHING NICE, DON'T SAY ANYTHING

Joining the dozen U.S. states where it's illegal to disparage fruits and vegetables, Philippine President Fidel Ramos ordered an end to an annual award for inept government officials named after a squash. He explained the "kalabasa" award dishonored the squash, which has become a successful export.

HATS IN THE RING

• To call attention to his campaign for the Curitiba, Brazil, City Council, Workers party candidate Julian Carlo Fagotti appeared in television commercials wearing only glasses and holding a campaign leaflet at his waist. "You work. They steal," Fagotti says in the nine-second spot. "You vote. They forget. They're the ones who should be ashamed."

• In another Brazilian municipal contest, the leading candidate for mayor of Pilar died mysteriously. Even more mysterious, the front-runner was a goat.

The week after a parade of fifty vehicles filled with the goat's supporters came under gunfire, its owner, Petrucio Maia, said he suspected a political rival had poisoned the goat, telling the *Folha de São Paulo* newspaper the animal "had a lot a foam in his mouth."

• In Idaho's Republican primary Dr. William Levinger took nearly a third of the vote against incumbent U.S. Representative Helen Chenoweth, then declared he would have done even better had he not suffered a manic episode during a taping of a local television talk show, been arrested for refusing to leave the studio, and spent three weeks at a psychiatric unit. "As much as I gave to the campaign," Levinger said, "all I come away with is the label of the guy who went crazy at the TV station."

• During the race for the Volusia County, Florida, Council, incumbent Lynne Plaskett skipped a council session to appear on the *Maury Povich Show* and announce that aliens from outer space cured her cancer twenty years ago. She said the night after learning she was dying of cancer of her lymph nodes, she heard a buzzing sound in her bedroom. The room filled with fog, she was levitated from her bed, and an eight-inch disk scanned her body three times. After Plaskett's revelation aired, she said she was deluged by calls that were "extremely positive," adding a few callers even had extraterrestrial tales of their own to share.

TO A TEE

When Tallahassee, Florida, Mayor Ron Weaver, who had been warned about following city golf course rules, tried to play on a city course before it opened for the day, maintenance worker Mike Osley turned on the sprinklers, driving the mayor from the course. Weaver admitted he was wrong, but Osley was suspended for a week without pay.

MILITARY INTELLIGENCE

When an army recruiter in Leesburg, Florida, told a woman trying to decide between the army and the navy that the navy couldn't guarantee her training for an intelligence job, a navy recruiter next door told the woman that indeed it could. An hour later three army sergeants, one swinging a crowbar, tried to trash the navy office. According to police, two marines rushed to help the navy. One was hit in the head with the crowbar, and the other got a black eye. Despite the army's victory, it lost the recruit. "She is signing up with us," Chief Petty Officer James Hutchins said. "She said she wasn't too impressed with the army."

SAFETY FIRST

• Workers at the Delaware Correctional Center preparing an outdoor gallows for the first execution by hanging in fifty years affixed nonskid safety strips to each of the twenty-three steps so convicted murderer Billy Bailey wouldn't slip as he climbed to the noose.

• When Oklahoma state prison officials found death row inmate Robert Brecheen, forty, unconscious from an overdose of sedatives in his cell, they rushed him to a hospital and had his stomach pumped. After Brecheen was revived, they returned him to the state penitentiary in McAlester, where he was executed by injection. "We have a responsibility for the health and welfare of our inmates," state corrections department spokesperson Jim Rabon said, "but we also have a responsibility to uphold the law." Under a 1986 U.S. Supreme Court ruling, condemned prisoners must be aware that they are being executed.

RUFFLED FEATHERS

India's social democratic Janata Dal party outraged its opponents in the eastern state of Bihar by capturing parrots and teaching them to recite political slogans at election meetings. The regional Jharkhand Mukti Morcha party demanded that the parrots be released, claiming Dal activists had clipped their wings to prevent them from escaping and starved them to force them to learn the slogans.

Rank Has Its Privileges

Lawmakers in California filed twice as many insurance claims in a four-year period as the average motorist, according to the *Orange County Register*. After reviewing state records, the paper reported that the lawmakers, who receive free cars and free insurance, submitted 163 accident claims, costing taxpayers about $500,000 in damage costs. State Senator Leroy Greene alone caused $61,452 in property and bodily injury damage to other motorists in two collisions that were determined to be his fault. Greene claimed he was distracted by the pressure of difficult bills, explaining, "It was a break in concentration. When I'm going through a legislative session, I'm endlessly trying to cogitate, ruminate and calculate. I'm always on a deadline and always got some problem facing me."

In the Dark

Sergeant Joseph J. Wollitz, a corrections officer at Florida's Duval County Jail, hatched a plan to scare two visiting juveniles into leading law-abiding lives by staging a fight among three inmates. When Wollitz asked for permission, a supervisor said no, but the three prisoners picked to take part in the ruse were never told. When the fake fight broke out, guards, including Wollitz, subdued the inmates with pepper spray. Wollitz was suspended by corrections director John Rutherford, who explained, "We can't ask inmates to perform violent acts with each other to impress anyone."

Silver Lining

After Lars Bildman, the chief executive of the pharmaceutical company Astra USA, was fired following accusations that he had replaced older women with younger, more attractive women, pressured female employees to have sex, and embezzled two million dollars, Astra board member Lars Ramqvist was quoted in the Swedish magazine *Maanadens Affaerer*: "Of course it's not good with sex scandals, but in the U.S. this has helped us get out Astra's name without having to pay expensive advertising fees."

Wrong Arm of the Law

• Out with forty members of his bachelor party, Drug Enforcement Administration agent Pete Sinclair, twenty-eight, objected to a five-dollar cover charge at a topless nightclub in Houston and got into a gunfight with the club's owner, Stavros Fotinopoulos, thirty-eight, and its manager, Lynn Clayton Turner, thirty-nine. Fotinopoulos was shot five times and Sinclair twice. Donald Ferrarone, DEA agent in charge in Houston, said Sinclair fired first.

• Boston Municipal Police officers Matthew Shea, twenty-six, Mark P. Atlee, twenty-nine, and Barry Maguire, twenty-seven, attending National Police Week ceremonies in Washington, D.C., to remember officers slain in the line of duty, were arrested after they ate at a

Georgetown restaurant, ran out on an eighteen-dollar bill, and threatened the manager when he ran after them to collect the money.

• At the previous year's National Police Week festivities, as many as a hundred New York City police officers, described by Police Commissioner William Bratton as "morons and nitwits," reportedly went on a drunken rampage at downtown Washington and suburban Virginia hotels. Witnesses said officers fired their weapons into the air, groped women, sprayed fire extinguishers into one hotel's ventilation system, stripped naked and took turns sliding down the beer-soaked center strip of an escalator, stole license plates, and set off fire alarms, causing middle-of-the-night evacuation of guests. Following a two-month investigation, one officer resigned after testing positive for cocaine and twenty-nine officers were reprimanded for taking their guns out of state.

SUSPICIOUS MINDS

• Police at Japan's Osaka airport stopped Ted Joffe, general manager of American Minerals, Inc., after the crew of his Thai Airways flight reported he had refused to eat his meal, "which could indicate that he swallowed drugs to smuggle into Japan." After Joffe was released, he commented, "Next time I'll stuff the meal into the seat pocket in front of me."

• British police who raided a pub in Loughborough, Lincolnshire, looking for a drug dealer nabbed an elderly gentleman who was in possession of a bag of white powder. The police let him go after he explained the powder was the ashes of his late wife, which he carried everywhere.

LEAP OF FAITH

Pedro Mosqueda, forty, decided he needed to do something "spectacular" to distance himself from two rivals hoping to become mayor of Maracay, Venezeula. A week before the election he bungee-jumped from a helicopter hovering five thousand feet above a crowd of fifteen thousand. Although the stunt sent his popularity soaring in opinion polls, he lost to Estela Roca de Azuaje when seventy percent of the voters stayed home. "Sometimes," Mosqueda lamented, "excitement and popularity aren't enough to win."

TRIGGER HAPPY

• Tony Dow, twenty-five, a sheriff's deputy in Butler County, Missouri, reported that a stranded motorist he stopped to help shot him in the arm. After a four-day search for the "scruffy-looking" gunman, Sheriff Fred Armes said Dow admitted he had actually wounded himself. After stopping on a rural road to urinate, he was throwing his service pistol in the air when he fumbled the throw and caught the gun in the crook of his arm, causing it to discharge.

• An unidentified twenty-six-year-old Spanish airport guard was hospitalized in Madrid after he shot himself while playing Russian roulette. Instead of having the customary one bullet in his revolver, the man had loaded four live rounds.

SECOND RATE

The Oklahoma state senate unanimously passed a bill combining a ban on bear wrestling with tougher penalties for spousal abuse. According to the measure, bear wrestling carries a maximum penalty of one year in jail and a five-thousand-dollar fine, while the penalty for abusing a current or former spouse is up to a year in jail and a two-thousand-dollar fine.

QUICK CASH

In Finland a computer system designed to shorten the length of time people have to wait in sub-zero temperatures at automated teller machines to withdraw cash turned out to be too fast. In some cases the security system in the program allowed customers only fifteen seconds to retrieve their cash before keeping it or their bank cards.

Shortcomings of Democracy

Tennessee state senators passed a measure urging homes, businesses, and schools in the state to post the Ten Commandments. "I think it's time to get back to the basics of morality in this country, which has traditionally been based in Judeo-Christian beliefs," said Ben Atchlet, R-Knoxville, sponsor of the bill. It passed, twenty-seven to one, because some of the lawmakers who voted for it said they couldn't afford to vote no. "I don't have time to explain to my 150,000 constituents about how this is America and this was about choice," declared Memphis Democrat Roscoe Dixon. "All they'll see is whether I voted for it or against it."

Opportunity Splashes

During a visit to Denver by Vice President Al Gore, Hamlet ("Chips") Barry III, chief of the city's water department, decided the South Platte River looked too shallow to serve as a backdrop for Gore's riverfront photo opportunity. He boosted the flow by releasing ninety-six million gallons of water, which the *Rocky Mountain News* reported was worth fifty-nine thousand dollars and could have supplied nearly three hundred families for a year. "I can defend it," Barry said. "When you have the river being showcased, you want it to look good."

THE ENEMY IS US

The army issued Bronze Stars to seven members of the Third Armored Cavalry Regiment for "meritorious achievement" during the Persian Gulf War, even though their achievement was mistakenly firing on U.S. soldiers, killing one and wounding another.

TAX REFORM

• Currituck County, North Carolina, board of education member Sam Walker insisted the reason he owes the state nearly $10,000 in back taxes is that he assumed he was exempt. "I'm an elected official," he explained. "I didn't know you had to pay taxes."

• California state Senator Don Rogers denied that he owed the federal government $150,000 in back taxes, declaring that because of the Fourteenth Amendment, he had a "white man's citizenship" and wasn't bound to pay taxes. Four years later the Palmdale Republican announced he was rescinding that declaration, explaining that he had taken the position in the first place after receiving some bad tax advice.

INGENUITY IN THE FACE OF ADVERSITY

According to documents released by the Food and Drug Administration, officials of U.S. Tobacco, the largest maker of chewing tobacco, advocated overcoming concerns about the dangers of smoking by marketing edible nicotine. "We must sell the use of tobacco in the mouth and appeal to young people," Vice President L. F. Bantle was quoted in the minutes of one meeting. "We hope to start a fad. The theme will be: 'Tobacco—too good to smoke.'" When a top scientist suggested creating a "swallowable chew: a confection with nicotine," the company considered the idea for two years before rejecting it.

LACKING SOUL

The Ford Motor Company in the United Kingdom acknowledged that it used a computer to change the races of five workers when their picture appeared on the cover of a company brochure. The original photo, which was used on the U.K. Ford Credit Options brochure, showed four blacks and a Sikh in a crowd with twenty-seven whites. *Advertising Age* reported that when the same photo was used in press and poster ads in Poland, the nonwhites were altered because according to the company, "the U.K. version obviously did not portray the ethnic mix in Poland." The photo was used in Poland until 1994, but then in 1997 the altered version was mistakenly used in a new credit brochure distributed in the U.K. Blaming "an administrative error," Ford issued formal apologies and checks for twenty-four hundred dollars to four of the nonwhite workers; the fifth had already left the company.

But It Works

U.S. District Judge Thad Heartfield halted the sale of the Quadro Positive Molecular Locator after government tests indicated the purported drug and explosives detector is a fake—even though several agencies using it insisted they were having good results with it. At least a thousand of the machines were sold or ordered by schools, prisons, airports, and law enforcement departments, which paid $395 to $8,000 each, according to FBI Agent Norman Townsend. The agency's analysis revealed it is nothing more than a hollow plastic box attached to a retractable transistor radio antenna. A purported "chip" inside turned out to be two pieces of plastic surrounding "a small piece of polymer-coated white paper, similar to a candy bar wrapper," Townsend said, adding that employees of the Quadro Corporation admitted the "chip" is "nothing more than photocopy paper."

Yo, Canada

• After Canadian Indians protested, Air Canada withdrew an advertisement depicting a spear-wielding

Indian chief in traditional garb standing next to a passenger in a business suit under the headline SITTING COMFORTABULL?

• Canadian Prime Minister Jean Chrétien, sixty-two, was formally charged with assault against a protester during a public event. Chrétien was making his way through a Flag Day crowd in Hull, Quebec, when Bill Clennett, forty-four, who was demonstrating against cuts in unemployment insurance, stood in the prime minister's path and shouted in French, "Chrétien to the unemployment line!" News cameras showed Chrétien grabbing the protester by the throat, wrenching his head, and shoving him aside. The Royal Canadian Mounted Police then wrestled Clennett to the ground. "This country's getting too violent," the *Globe and Mail* of Toronto said of the episode. "You'd never catch an American president doing that kind of thing."

CANDID CAMERA

• When an alarm went off at Naomi's Busy Mart in Buffalo, New York, police responded and searched the convenience store, which was closed. Not realizing they were being videotaped by the store's security camera, one of the two officers began "taking snack food and eating it," according to the store owner's lawyer, Glenn Murray, who said that in one scene the officer "looks like he's got a hot dog in his mouth." After the police left, the tape shows two burglars breaking into the store and stealing cigarettes, lottery tickets, and other items. The police again responded to the alarm, this time with reinforcements. Again the camera caught them helping themselves, Murray said. "You see three of them laughing and feasting and drinking."

• South Carolina Highway Patrol Lance Corporal W. H. Beckwith was fired for yanking a speeding suspect out of her car, throwing her to the ground, cursing her, and threatening to cut off her clothes. The chief evidence against Beckwith was a tape from his own patrol car's video camera, which turns on with the car's lights and sirens and keeps running until the lights are turned off. Public Safety Director Boykin Rose said the tape showed Beckwith "violating every procedure in the book."

SPELLING COUNTS

• Randolph Espinosa, an ex-Secret Service agent who protected former President Reagan for thirteen years, was sentenced to sixteen months in jail after pleading guilty to selling baseballs and other souvenirs with fake autographs. Espinosa admitted selling nearly three hundred baseballs with Reagan's signature, explaining that some were forged but some were signed by Reagan as he sat by the pool at his Rancho del Cielo near Santa Barbara. Espinosa also sold bogus signatures

of Presidents Bush and Kennedy and former first lady
Jacqueline Kennedy Onassis. According to Assistant
U.S. Attorney Marc Harris, the scam unraveled when a
collector noticed that Jacqueline Kennedy's "signature"
was misspelled.

• A Danish court ordered Pia Agergaard to pay
ninety-one dollars a week for refusing to change the
spelling of her son's first name, Christophpher, after
ruling that spelling the name with *phph* is illegal.

FULL OF HOT AIR

Authorities in Canberra, Australia, said they were con-
sidering taxing animal flatulence as part of the city's
plan to cut greenhouse gas emissions twenty percent
by the year 2005.

FOOD FOR THOUGHT

• The Food and Drug Administration approved
olestra for potato chips, crackers, and other snack
foods despite considerable evidence that the fat substi-
tute causes abdominal cramping and loose stools.

• Canada's Health Ministry informed Eskimos that
dangerous pesticides carried to the Arctic from the

Third World by wind and ocean currents have contaminated seal and whale blubber, making it unsafe to eat. But the ministry told the natives that they should continue eating the blubber because even contaminated, it is considered at least as healthy as the standard North American diet of processed and junk food.

BITING THE HAND THAT FEEDS

When the Raleigh, North Carolina, City Council indicated it would approve rezoning land to allow a restaurant to open, only one potential neighbor objected: the North Carolina Restaurant Association. The trade group cited parking and unspecified other problems as reasons it didn't want the restaurant next door.

GOVERNMENT INTELLIGENCE

• U.S. spy satellites, focusing on targets chosen by eleven military and intelligence agencies, gather information faster than experts can analyze it. The *Washington Post* reported that given the choice between collecting less or analyzing more, the intelligence community opted to upgrade its processing operations. The goal, CIA Director John M. Deutch said, was to give U.S. forces "a unique dominant battlefield awareness." To further this aim, the House Permanent Select Intelligence Committee budgeted two million dollars to finance a study of "all national and theater imagery-collection platforms, all types of imagery products" and "all imagery exploitation software packages to better support targeting of precision weapons."

• Meanwhile, the *New York Times* reported a team of auditors sent by Deutch discovered that the National Reconnaissance Office, the secret agency that controls the nation's four or five sophisticated spy satellites, had lost track of more than two billion dollars in secret bank accounts. According to one intelligence committee aide, the misplaced money resulted from a severe bookkeeping problem that grew from a lack of accountability created by the agency's extraordinary secrecy. Congressional oversight of the agency is ineffective, the aide said, because few members of Congress understand the highly technical language of spy satellites or know what they're approving when they authorize billions of dollars a year in secret spending.

• In Germany, following the arrest of three men for trying to sneak nearly a pound of weapons-grade plutonium into Germany in 1994, that country's Federal Intelligence Service was accused of causing the very smuggling it uncovered. Martin Schulz, an investigator for the European Parliament, said the incident was not the first episode of nuclear contraband that had turned out to be a case of the tiger chasing its tail. "In every case in which a buyer has surfaced, government authorities were the buyers," he told German television.

"Those who want to combat the market are the same ones who have really created it."

SPEND ALL YOU WANT, WE'LL PRINT MORE

• Contractors building a $3.6 million control tower at the Redmond, Oregon, airport complained about the government's insistence that they install a $5,000 vacuum system to clean a five-hundred-square-foot space. The Federal Aviation Administration specified a two-horsepower, 230-volt, three-phase, sixty-hertz vacuum, which Steven McGinnis, operations manager for the project's mechanical contractor, called "just huge overkill. I mean, they could go down and buy themselves a $100 Hoover and do the same thing." FAA spokesperson Tim Pile defended the requirement, explaining, "The engineers have built a number of these towers, and I think they know what they're doing."

• The opening of the new control tower at Washington's National Airport had to be delayed several months after it was discovered that the consoles that had been installed prevented controllers shorter than five feet five from seeing parts of the ramp and taxiways.

UNDOMESTICATED

Urinating dogs in Tiburon, California, were blamed for shorting out a twenty-thousand-dollar sidewalk lighting system, costing the town two hundred dollars a month. Public works director Tony Iacoppi said canines can't resist the foot-tall lights, which illuminate the downtown Shoreline Park walkway. "All it takes is one dog to pee on it, and then it's over," he said. "Every dog in the world wants to pee on them. They are corroding all the fixtures and all the wiring."

NAME RECOGNITION

Three months after Saskatchewan gas station owner Dick Assman had appeared on television's *Late Show with David Letterman* because of his name, pollsters Angus Reid said its survey showed 1.1 million Canadians now knew who Assman was and would vote for him should he run for public office.

SEER SUCKERS

• The CIA confirmed that for twenty years the government secretly used psychics to gather intelligence information. The extrasensory perception spying operation, code-named Stargate, cost taxpayers twenty million dollars. It employed as many as six psychics, who were consulted more than two hundred times for remote viewing, using ESP to provide information from distant sites, such as helping hunt down Libyan leader Colonel Muammar Gadhafi, finding plutonium in North Korea, and aiding drug enforcement agencies.

• Former Orange County, California, finance director Eileen Walsh told a grand jury that Robert L. Citron, seventy, the former county treasurer whose ill-fated investments pushed the county into bankruptcy, had relied on interest rate forecasts from a mail-order astrologer and regularly consulted a psychic.

• Thomas J. Tobin, thirty-five, police chief of Camden Point, Missouri, resigned after being accused of making as many as 280 calls to a psychic hot line during a four-month period. The calls, which cost taxpayers twenty thousand dollars, lasted from four to forty minutes.

STRANGE BEDFELLOWS

A loophole in state law let three convicted felons run for sheriff in three Mississippi counties. They won. "This really makes us look kind of dumb," Public Safety Commissioner Jim Ingram said. "I can only believe that many voters did not know the situation." State Attorney General Mike Moore, noting that state law prohibits anyone convicted of a felony from bearing arms, said any of the three new sheriffs who carried a gun would be arrested.

CRIME AND PUNISHMENT

The government of Chile spent $2.5 million to build a luxury prison north of Santiago designed to hold only two inmates: former secret police boss General Manuel Contreras and his colleague Pedro Espinoza. Officials said a fifteen-foot wall built around the facility is intended not so much to keep the men inside as to keep snooping reporters out.

WE'RE FROM THE GOVERNMENT, WE'RE HERE TO HELP

• Using a gill net to catch illegally introduced lake trout at Yellowstone National Park backfired, according to federal biologists. The net, which kills the fish it catches, snared only 4 lake trout compared with 150 cutthroat, the species the biologists are trying to save.

• Fish and Wildlife Service scientists in Tacoma, Washington, announced plans to kill about forty sea ducks called surf scoters to try to determine why their numbers are declining.

• Thailand's tax department announced that a new levy on products and services that harm the environment includes massage parlors because they provide a luxury service that wastes water.

DON'T ASK, DON'T TELL

After President Clinton arranged a meeting with forty or so homosexual elected officials to smooth out his administration's relationship with the gay community, White House guards greeted the state senators and representatives, city councillors, judges, and other officials by putting on rubber gloves. They explained they were protecting themselves. Echoing the reaction of some colleagues, Mike Nelson, an alderman from Carrboro, North Carolina, said he was "offended and disappointed" by the assumption "that everyone who is gay has AIDS."

CAPTIVE AUDIENCE

Sheriff's department officials in Dallas County, Texas, complained about the efficiency of the smoke removal system at the new thirty-three-hundred-bed jail that opened in 1993. About forty times a day, they said, prisoners set off the highly sensitive system by blowing cigarette smoke at detectors. In sealing off areas, the system causes doors to slam so quickly that two guards had already been injured.

FOOT-IN-MOUTH DISEASE

During a debate by the North Carolina House Appropriations Committee on a proposal to eliminate a state abortion fund for poor women, Representative Henry Aldridge, seventy-one, intended to apologize for earlier remarks implying that victims of rape or incest are sexually promiscuous when he expressed the belief that rape victims don't get pregnant. "The facts show that people who are raped—who are truly raped—the juices don't flow, the body functions don't work, and they don't get pregnant. Medical authorities agree this is a rarity, if ever."

Aldridge later defended his comments against criticism: "To get pregnant, it takes a little cooperation. And there ain't much cooperation with rape."

GOOD CLEAN FUN

In England, Labour Councillor Ben Summerskill accused undercover council officials and police of going "beyond the call of duty" after they insisted they visited a massage parlor seventeen times to make absolutely sure they had enough evidence. Noting that they were given "amateurish massages" by scantily clad young

women before being offered sex, which they politely
refused, the inspectors insisted that the seventeen vis-
its, costing $3,160, were necessary to prove that it was
the owner, not the individual masseuses, who were
breaking the law.

SPEAKING THEIR MIND

Representative Mark Souder, R-Indiana, compared people in Kentucky and Tennessee with Branch Davidian
cult leader David Koresh. After telling a reporter from
the Fort Wayne, Indiana, *Journal-Gazette* that the only
law the FBI clearly established Koresh broke was having sex with consenting minors, Souder asked, "Do you
send tanks and government troops into the large sec-
tions of Kentucky and Tennessee and other places
where such things occur?" Noting that Koresh viewed
himself as married to the women, the freshman Republican accused the government of "sending tanks in to
enforce polygamy laws."

HEY, HE'S CURED

A New York state mental hospital sent wife killer
Alphonso Pecou, forty-three, for "spiritual counseling"
and received a bill for twelve thousand dollars for an exorcism. The Reverend Alpha O. Bundu, self-described

primate and pastor of the United Church of Salvation, billed the state for dunking Pecou in a ritual mineral water bath and anointing him with olive oil, then praying over him to drive out demons. Pecou, a Panama native with what the state Office of Mental Health describes as an "extreme attachment to a Caribbean religion, slashed his wife to death with a machete and set her on fire in front of his four children because he felt she was insufficiently devout." "We try to be culturally sensitive, but we indicated that exorcism was a nontraditional treatment modality that was not billable," said Robert Spoor, a spokeperson for the Mental Health Office, which paid Bundu five hundred dollars, an amount based on the usual rate for more conventional spiritual counseling by a priest or rabbi.

HEALTH SCARE

After surgeon Rolando Sanchez amputated the wrong leg of a patient at University Community Hospital in Tampa, Florida, the hospital started a new policy of writing the word *No* on patients' limbs that are not supposed to be removed.

TAX DOLLARS AT WORK

After fourteen years of development and manufacture, including six years of test flights, the government

announced that the B-2 stealth bomber had advanced
to the point where it can evade enemy radar—so long
as it doesn't rain. According to a draft report by the
General Accounting Office, raindrops distort the skin
of the eight-hundred-million-dollar aircraft, causing it
to become more detectable. The report, obtained by
the *New York Times*, also noted that the aircraft's own
radar, intended to let the plane hug the ground as
it flies, can't distinguish between rain and a wall or
mountain.

LENDING NATURE A HAND

The U.S. Forest Service proposed spending eighteen
thousand dollars to paint rocks along a scenic highway
through Washington's Cascade Mountains. The agency
explained that it wanted to dye the rocks gray and
brown so they would look more natural to tourists.

NO SURPRISE

• Congressional auditors reported they cannot
verify Internal Revenue Service tax collections for 1994
because IRS records are in disarray. "IRS did not know
and we could not determine if the reported amounts
were correct," General Accounting Office auditors wrote,
according to Senator John Glenn, D-Ohio, who requested

the audit. He likened the IRS system to "keeping your lifetime records in a shoe box under the bed." Agency spokesperson Frank Keith blamed the problem on a thirty-year-old computer system.

• According to the GAO audit, the IRS "cannot reconcile the accounting records it keeps on individual taxpayers with the $1.4 trillion in revenues it collected or the $122 billion in refunds it paid." Further, the IRS had no idea of just how accurate is its estimate that it's owed $113 billion in overdue taxes. It also couldn't accurately verify how it spent $3 billion.

• The IRS did manage to complete an internal review in April 1994 that revealed that 16,800 IRS employees who owed taxes for 1993 either paid or filed late or failed to file returns at all. Six months later an IRS computer check of 110,665 employees found 733 still had not filed 1993 tax returns, and 4,192 owed back taxes, averaging more than $2,000. Tax lawyer George Guttman, who reported the IRS findings in the weekly paper *Tax Notes*, concluded, "In general, IRS employees are not significantly more compliant than taxpayers as a whole."

GOTTA RUN

• Wendy Lee Gramm, wife of then Republican presidential candidate Senator Phil Gramm of Texas, announced that she would campaign for her husband by in-line skating 213 miles across western Maryland in July 1996. She covered 105 miles in two days before collapsing from heat exhaustion and spending two nights in the hospital.

• John Anderson, thirty-seven, of Berkeley Springs, West Virginia, placed an ad in the *Morgan Messenger* announcing he was seeking his state's gubernatorial nomination. A week later Anderson took out a second ad retracting the first, explaining, "I had just been discharged from the hospital under heavy medication."

LITTLE THINGS MEAN A LOT

Brazil's government canceled a five-million-dollar safe sex campaign featuring a talking penis after two groups complained. The Catholic Church objected because the television ads promote condom use, which Raimundo Damasceno Assis of the National Council of Brazilian Bishops said encourages sexual promiscuity. People named Braulio protested because that was the chatty organ's moniker. Braulio is a common family and first name, but Health Minister Adib Jatene cited a survey showing it also is a common nickname for a penis.

First to threaten a lawsuit was São Paulo law professor Braulio Monte, Jr. He insisted that having a talking penis named Braulio on TV could damage him professionally.

GLITCHES

• Bell Atlantic spent $100,300 to print and mail postcards notifying 388,000 telephone customers in western Virginia that their area code was changing from 703 to 540, but the postcards went to business and residential customers in northern Virginia, where the area code isn't changing. Company spokesperson Paul Miller blamed a computer glitch and estimated correcting the mistake would cost Bell Atlantic two to three times the original amount.

• The Marine Spill Response Corporation agreed to pay Ventura County, California, and the state department of fish and game a total of $73,000 to settle a civil lawsuit filed by the county district attorney over a spill of 383 gallons of diesel fuel into Port Hueneme Harbor. The fuel leaked from a new company ship designed to clean up oil spills.

FIRST THINGS FIRST

Plans to have John Paul II become the first pope to appear before a joint session of Congress during his 1995 visit to the United States were scuttled when church officials said the only date the pontiff was available was October 9, the federal holiday of Columbus Day. "If there is one thing members of Congress can count on, and there may be only one thing, it is that we will not be in session on federal holidays," Tony Blankley, a spokesperson for House Speaker Newt Gingrich, told the *Baltimore Sun.* "I can't imagine anything, short of war, that could cause us to change that."

ELECTION FOLLIES

• Ken Barnett, a candidate for sheriff of Henry County, Virginia, aired commercials showing his opponent, incumbent Sheriff H. Frank Cassell, side by side with Adolf Hitler and referring to deputies as "goose-stepping Gestapo." Appalled at being likened to Hitler, Cassell won reelection but complained the three to one margin over Barnett wasn't enough.

• Battling for the Democratic nomination in the race to succeed Senator Bob Packwood, R-Oregon, Representative Peter DeFazio accused an opponent, Representative Ron Wyden, of having run over a dog twenty years earlier. Wyden acknowledged the deed, explaining, "I felt really bad about it and still remember it to this day." He added: "It's kind of hard to see what this has to do with running for the U.S. Senate."

GOVERNMENT IN ACTION

U.S. Representative Joe Knollenberg, R-Michigan, wrote to the Department of Agriculture on behalf of Oink-Oink

Inc., a Detroit company that the USDA was allowing to buy pork penises "for use as a pet treat." After several months, however, the USDA began to dye the raw penises green. Oink-Oink thought the green dye would make the product unappealing and discontinued it, taking a hundred-thousand-dollar loss and enraging dog owners who loved the treat, called Pork Tenderloins. A USDA spokesperson explained that the penises were dyed green as a warning to keep humans from snacking on them.

Tough Lesson

The Swedish government announced the country's six-year-old children would be given $7.70 each to spend as they chose. The point of the one-time gift, officials explained, was to teach them that once the money is spent, it's gone.

Down Under Down Under

A New Zealand town council announced that it was charging more to bury large people. Explaining that the cost of oversize graves at Porirua's Whenua Tapu cemetery would rise thirty percent, John Seddon, the council's chief executive, dismissed complaints from Pacific Islanders that the surcharge is discriminatory because they tend to grow bigger than other people.

METAPHORS FOR OVERSPENDING

• The Pentagon canceled its Hunter Short-Range Unmanned Aerial Vehicle—a twenty-four-foot propeller-driven drone—after all nine prototypes crashed in separate desert tests. The failed venture cost $600 million. Software problems were so bad that some of the drones, programmed to fly in a straight line, instead went up and began flying in circles.

• In 1985 the Pentagon ordered two Henry J. Kaiser–class oil tankers for the navy. The initial contract for the two totaled $222 million and was awarded even though the navy suspected that the manufacturer's bid was "overly optimistic." Problems at the first contracting firm forced the navy to raise the contract to $331 million, but finally it decided to abandon that firm when it developed financial problems and ran out of money.

After lobbying by New York Yankees owner George Steinbrenner, the navy awarded the balance of the contract to a second company owned by Steinbrenner. Since it was in Florida, the half-finished ships had to be prepared to be moved to Tampa. That alone cost $10 million. Once they reached Florida, after one ship was damaged by running aground off North Carolina, the new contractor balked at the ships' poor condition. The navy then awarded an additional $45 million for the completion of the ships. Finally, in 1993, the navy terminated the contract over "financial and performance" problems at the Florida company. In 1995 the ships were towed to Newport News, Virginia, where they sit half finished and rusting after the government spent $450 million.

EVERYTHING YOU ALWAYS SUSPECTED IS TRUE

Public Health Service physician James D. Felsen acknowledged that he was being paid $117,000 per year, including a $15,000 bonus, for doing nothing—and had been for three years. Felsen told the *Washington Post* that each day he drank a cup of coffee, read the newspaper, checked his mail, and telephoned friends. He pointed to a styrofoam coffee cup arch—running up one wall, across the ceiling of his office and down the opposite wall—which he had created over the years, placing each day's coffee cup inside the previous day's.

Felsen wound up in this position after disagreeing with his superiors over his management of a Public Health Service program. After allegations were made from both sides, an investigation dragged on for years. Felsen claimed that he was being punished by being given his do-nothing assignment.

One month after the story appeared, the agency placed Felsen on paid administrative leave. Two months after that it decided that there "was insufficient evidence to involuntarily retire him" and reassigned him to a new program.

DUH, I WONDER WHY THEY KILLED ALL THOSE PRIESTS AND NUNS

Military intelligence manuals used by instructors to train Latin America military officers at the U.S. Army's School of the Americas in Panama and (since 1984) at Fort Benning, Georgia, advocated the use of extortion, torture, and execution as legitimate tools to use against domestic insurgents. As for recruiting and controlling informants, the manuals recommended "fear, payment of bounties for enemy dead, beatings, false imprisonment, executions, and the use of truth serum." Despite longtime claims by the army that the curriculum encouraged the creation of professional officers and spread democracy throughout Central America, military officers who have been held responsible for flagrant human rights abuses and murders in their respective countries are among the school's graduates.

The existence of the manuals was revealed only in 1996. The army claimed that it had addressed the problem in 1992 with an internal investigation and had ceased using the material in 1991. The 1992 investigation also discovered that thousands of copies of the manuals had been distributed to thousands of military officers in eleven South and Central American countries over the years.

How About "Should We Pay for Any More of These?"

Since 1970 the federal government's Consumer Information Center has produced thousands of educational pamphlets, including such recent favorites as *How to Buy Meat*, *Helping Your Child with Homework*, *How to Buy Fresh Fruit*, and *Should You Go on a Diet?*

GUESS IT WORKED

Air traffic controller Douglas Hartman filed a sexual harassment suit, charging that he and other men at a workshop sponsored by the Federal Aviation Administration were forced to run a gauntlet of women who touched their buttocks, fondled their crotches, and made lewd sexual comments as part of an exercise to increase awareness about sexual harassment in the workplace.

BEATS FLYING TO A HUB

Ten air force reservists flew a C-141 cargo jet from Washington State to North Carolina and Indiana and then back home in 1995, claiming it was part of a training mission. The reservists had coincidentally arranged to attend professional basketball games near both bases that weekend. They also flew with a government-owned van in the plane's cargo bay, which they unloaded in Indiana to drive to the game, sixty miles away. The incident was reported when the crew pulled their plane up next to the Seattle Supersonics plane at the Charlotte airport and were overheard by an airport worker saying that they were there to see the game. They also saw the Supersonics play in Indiana the next night.

SWEAT THE DETAILS

The *Washington Post* published a memo from the IRS counsel's finance and management division notifying employees that the deputy chief counsel "does not want to receive any memorandums, letters, etc. with hyphenated words." A second memo specified that "the word [nonbargaining] is the word that the deputy chief counsel does not want hyphenated. But as a rule she does not want hyphenated words in letters, memos, unless it is at the end of the sentence. PLEASE pass this information on to persons in your branch."

ON INHALING EVERY DAY

Despite the Clinton administration's efforts to oppose initiatives passed in California and Arizona to allow the medical use of marijuana, the federal government already grows it and provides it to eight patients. Since 1976 the University of Mississippi has grown pot under a contract with the National Institute on Drug Abuse. Overseen by the Food and Drug Administration, the Compassionate Investigative New Drug program provides marijuana to relieve symptoms associated with epilepsy, cancer, glaucoma, multiple sclerosis, and some rare genetic diseases. The program began with thirteen patients. Five are now dead. The remaining eight receive up to three hundred marijuana cigarettes per month.

But They're the Really, Really Strong Plastic Bags

An internal Department of Energy study in 1994 determined that there were twenty-six metric tons of plutonium scraps and fragments in the department's nuclear weapons facilities that posed "significant hazards to workers, the public and the environment." Plutonium was found to be stored in more than 64,387 individual plastic bags, metal food cans, canisters, drums, and glass bottles. Some of the canisters are unsealed, and some of the drums are unmarked—and some have started to break or decompose.

Ready Kilowatt's Packin'!

According to a Department of Energy inspector general's report, the department's laboratories have been stockpiling weapons, including 84 grenade launchers, 493 submachine guns, 457 shotguns, 5,168 handguns, and 90 armored personnel carriers—an average of 4 weapons per lab security officer.

Commonplace Overspending

The General Accounting Office determined that the Pentagon's Military Sealift Command spent $260 apiece to repair ten table lamps on board a ship while the cost of buying new lamps was only $210 each.

MINK IF YA GOT 'EM

The army spent more than five million dollars to find out if minks get sick when they are fed a nerve gas by-product. The testing is to determine whether state environmental standards can be reduced for the cleanup of the Rocky Mountain Arsenal. Reducing the standards means the army can save about seven million dollars for its part of the cleanup. After spending about eighty-one hundred dollars per mink, it was determined that the by-product did not harm the health of the minks. However, the project director said, "If you look at what we spent per mink, the cost was terrible. At some point, you wonder why all this is necessary. When you think about spending tax dollars on something, you wonder if there aren't better things than this."

THE ANSWERS: RUN, MOVE, AND A REAL PISSED-OFF LOOK

The interest group Citizens Against Government Waste reported that the National Institute of Mental Health funded studies such as "Israeli Reactions to Scud Attacks During the Gulf War" (cost: $16,913) and "Human Response to Repeated Floods" (cost: $76,971) as well

as a $104,055 study to determine how people communi-
cate using facial expressions. According to the grant
proposal on the last one, "It can be difficult for people
to control their facial expressions because they cannot
see their own faces."

WHEN BEING ON HOLD IS DEDUCTIBLE

The General Accounting Office reported that between
1989 and 1994, the "percentage of taxpayers' calls that
IRS assistors [*sic*] answered ranged from 50 percent
in fiscal 1989 to 23 percent in fiscal year 1994." The
agency found that the problem is not just at tax time
but year-round. The annual number of "abandoned"
calls—those who dial into the IRS assistance system
and never receive an answer—rose to 6 million in 1994
from 2.4 million in 1989.

WE'RE LOOKING INTO RUMORS OF
SOMETHING CALLED TEAPOT DOME

The Federal Election Commission spent seven years
investigating the 1988 presidential campaign of former
President George Bush, trying to determine the legality
of some contributions received by his campaign organization (namely, money received from the National
Republican Committee and eighteen state party com-
mittees to pay for sixteen trips). By December 1995 the

FEC determined that first, the campaign had received $223,000 in illegal contributions and second, it was too late to penalize the campaign. Instead it sent the campaign's lawyers a letter warning them to "take steps to ensure that this kind of activity does not occur in the future."

HEY, STUPID!

A U.S. Forest Service announcement for a job opening for a fire prevention technician read in part, "Only applicants who do not meet the [Office of Personnel Management] qualifications requirements will be considered."

IT'S MY TURN TO GO KABOOM

The House Armed Services Committee conducted a survey of U.S. military units around the world to determine how various commands dealt with dwindling funds in the last month of the government's fiscal year. Among the findings was that a battalion of the Second Armored Division at Fort Hood, Texas, decided to save fuel costs by conducting tank battle exercises in a new way. The tank platoons would drive out to the battlefield and park. The crews would then dismount but stay in a group, pretending to be in their tanks. Then they would proceed with their training exercises, walking

around the battlefield, all still pretending to be in their
tanks.

Ask About Our Special Deals

The prices of spare parts for the air force's C-17 transport plane rose dramatically once the main contractor,
the McDonnell Douglas Corporation, took over the
manufacture of some parts after it became concerned
about meeting deadlines, according to a General Accounting Office report. A door hook originally produced by a subcontractor for $389 rose to $8,842. A
door hinge that originally cost $31 from the subcon-
tractor jumped to $2,187. An aluminum handle went
from $60 to $1,206. The GAO report looked only at
thirty-two of the C-17's four million parts.

Sisyphus, Call Your Office

The federal government spent $5.6 billion in 1995 to
maintain the security of top secret documents. (That
figure does not reflect the money spent by the Central
Intelligence Agency, which did not make its costs public.) That is just for maintenance, with only less than
one percent involved in the cost of declassification of
these documents. By law all documents more than
twenty-five years old are ready for declassification.
Current estimates are that more than one billion pages
are awaiting declassification.

WAIT!

A 1996 report found that construction was continuing on several military installations that either had been closed for years or were on the list of facilities due to be closed shortly. Thus, at Fort Sheridan near Chicago, a facility that had been shut for three years, the construction was scheduled to begin for a $3.3 million addition to some buildings used by the navy. In Orlando, Florida, the navy spent $13 million for a dining hall and personnel center on a base that was to be closed within two years. The San Diego Naval Training Center opened a new $5.1 million chapel to hold graduation exercises for its last class; the center was closing. A Pentagon official explained that according to the terms of some of its construction contracts, it's more expensive to break the contract and stop construction than to go ahead with it.

BUT YOU CAN EAT OFF THE FLOORS

The chief of maintenance at the Federal Reserve, who oversees the mailroom, food services, procurement, and security, has an annual salary of $163,800. That's higher than the $148,400 that cabinet secretaries earn and more than the salary of even the Federal Reserve chairman himself.

AND IT JULIENNES-FRIES

The Department of Energy prepared an environmental impact report on various proposals to use the government's Nevada test site (home of atomic weapons testing) that cost the department ten million dollars to produce. The first printing of two thousand copies was a ten-volume set weighing more than fifteen pounds. It includes, among other things, a 160-page appendix listing the names used by three Native American tribes for 170 animals and 364 plants in the region. It also has an appendix listing the names of everyone on the initial distribution list to receive the report.

FROM SMALL THINGS, BIG THINGS ONE DAY COME

In 1986 managers at the Pentagon's Defense Finance and Accounting Service Center in Denver determined that they had miscalculated the pay of 201,851 air force retirees for the previous two years. Because of the error, retirees each received one or two dollars extra each month that they were not entitled to. The managers then decided that the computer program used to generate the checks needed to be reprogrammed to correct the error. They finally got around to it in 1992. The cumulative cost to the taxpayers of the unattended problem over the nine years was estimated at sixteen million dollars.

PACK RATS

The General Accounting Office reported in 1995 that the Department of Defense had managed to reduce its unneeded inventory from forty-three billion to thirty-six billion dollars over the previous three years. However, the agency noted that the Pentagon had "wasted billions of dollars on excess supplies, burdened itself with the need to store them, and failed to acquire the tools or expertise needed to manage them effectively." Said Delaware Senator William Roth: "I am appalled that over one trillion dollars of the Department of Defense's inventory cannot be accounted for. How do you lose a tank?"

WHO YOU GONNA CALL?

Investigators at the Department of Agriculture determined that prison inmates in at least five states made more than five hundred collect third-party calls, many long distance, from their places of incarceration, and successfully billed them to the department's Washington, D.C., headquarters. The calls occurred during late 1994 and throughout 1995, with the majority coming from the District of Columbia's Lorton Correctional Complex. Indiana Senator Richard Lugar, chairman of the Senate Agriculture Committee, said that it was "unclear why USDA staff would accept collect calls from anyone in the first place, let alone calls from correctional facilities." He also suggested that other federal departments may also have been duped.

WORK SUCKS. ANYTHING ELSE?

The National Endowment for the Humanities awarded more than $4.2 million as part of a program called a National Conversation, an initiative to encourage Americans to get together and talk in structured discussion groups about what it means to be an American. The idea was originally suggested by the NEH chairman Sheldon Hackney, who termed the subject "elusive" but "very important." The largest individual grant under the project was $383,000 to the American Library Association to run a hundred conversations in twenty states about citizens' views of work as part of an examination of American values.

IT'S THE NEW MOTHER NATURE TAKIN' OVER

In an effort to increase the supply of nutrients in the water for the growth of younger salmon, Oregon's Department of Fish and Wildlife started stocking twenty-six coastal streams with dead salmon.

BOTTOM GUN

Navy investigators revealed that a crash of an F-14 jet fighter was caused when the plane's pilot and navigator removed their helmets and oxygen masks and put on their cloth garrison caps and posed saluting pilots in a nearby plane who were taking their picture. The two died from a lack of oxygen after they also shut off the plane's oxygen supply to cut down on the noise during the "stunt." By the time they turned it back on, it was too late.

PEOPLE WHO DON'T GET OUT MUCH

During the 1996 GOP presidential primary campaign, just before the Iowa caucuses, a group opposed to gay rights charged that candidate Malcolm S. ("Steve") Forbes, Jr., had a work of art by the artist Robert Mapplethorpe aboard his yacht. "Why is Steve Forbes patronizing a homoerotic artist?" an Iowa official asked the group. "He is spending millions in Iowa to tell us he is conservative, but why does he continue to own and display works by Mapplethorpe?" A Forbes spokesperson noted that the work of art in question is by Mapplethorpe and, like the other works of art aboard the yacht, is a seascape.

IMMODEST PROPOSAL

Montana State Senator Jim Burnett drafted a bill mandating public spanking on the bare buttocks as the punishment for vandalism. The penalty would apply to both juveniles and adults.

HEY, THOSE PANTS ARE ON FIRE

• Republican Representative Wes Cooley of Oregon, who was forced to retire after one term amid allegations that he had lied about his military service and his marriage, made a speech to the Northwest Forestry Association suggesting that one reason to return the GOP to control of the House in the 1996 elections was a report that if the Democrats came back to power, they would appoint former Speaker Jim Wright to head a new ethics office. Cooley openly referred to his source during the speech, holding aloft the April 1 edition of *Roll Call*, the newspaper that covers happenings in Congress. Apparently Cooley was unaware that the entire front page of that day's edition was one big April Fool's joke crammed with bogus headlines. If you turned the page, you found the real front page inside.

When a reporter approached him days later for a comment about the incident, Cooley said, "The only thing that is keeping you from getting your nose busted is that you are a lady."

• During a news conference to address allegations that he had falsified his record of military service in the Korean War, Cooley said that "Sergeant Major Poppy" was the only person who could verify the record of his service because the paper records had burned in a government warehouse fire. Poppy "was with me, and he's deceased, they tell me," said Cooley. Days later reporters found that Poppy was alive, and he said Cooley's claims of service were "a lie." Poppy had left Korea in 1951 before Cooley entered the army and served with him later in this country.

WHY NOT THE BEST?

• During the 1996 Democratic congressional primary, voters in Wyoming had to consider U.S. Senate hopeful Mickey Kalinay and U.S. House candidate V. Worth Christie, among others. Kalinay had an Internet home page for his campaign that advertised, "I have no political experience. In fact I have no experience at all that would recommend me for this position. What I have is . . . the dream of building a tower up into space. . . . I think I can wander around Wyoming saying our country needs a dream and that a tower into space would work very well for that dream."

For his part, Christie disclosed that he had served fifteen months in prison thirty years before and that his unique understanding of the criminal justice system and serving time in prison would allow him to go to Congress with a valuable perspective on the issue of crime.

• Another congressional candidate was Jessi Winchester, fifty-four, of Nevada, a former prostitute who had worked in a legal brothel. The brothels opposed her entry into the race, fearing adverse publicity. Said George Flint, lobbyist for the Nevada Brothel Association: "There are a lot of women in the state that have turned tricks. We've never suggested that any of them run for public office."

• In Arkansas, self-described former "groupie" Connie Hamzy decided to run as an independent candidate for a House seat. Hamzy is most famous for being immortalized as "Sweet, Sweet Connie" in Grand Funk Railroad's 1973 hit song "We're an American Band." Hamzy's campaign slogan was "I'm Not a Lawyer."

• Mistress Madison, a California dominatrix, entered the primary race for a U.S. House seat as a candidate for Ross Perot's Reform party. Madison runs a phone sex service and the Mistress Madison Slave Cave. She said she chose to compete for the Reform party's nomination because she found the Republican party too conservative and the Democratic party too liberal.

SEEING IS BELIEVING
Massachusetts State Representative John Cox introduced legislation to exempt blind veterans from paying a sales tax on motor vehicles.

THEY KNOW WHAT THEY LIKE
Voters in Friendsville, Maryland, reelected Mayor Spencer Schlosnagle to a fifth term despite two convictions while in office for exposing himself in public.

NOT A GOOD START
In 1995 the Missouri legislature passed a bill to reduce state paperwork. The bill weighed five pounds and was 1,012 pages long.

WAXING NOSTALGIC

Alabama State Senator Charles Davidson withdrew from the 1996 Republican congressional primary race after the uproar following a speech he made on the floor of the state senate arguing that slavery was justified by the Bible. "The incidence of abuse, rape, broken homes and murder are 100 times greater, today, in the housing projects than they ever were on the slave plantations in the Old South," he claimed. "The truth is that nowhere on the face of the earth, in all of time, were servants better treated or better loved than they were in the Old South by white, black, Hispanic, and Indian slave owners."

LIVING ON LOVE STREET

• A Kentucky prison inmate succeeded in persuading the governors of six states to proclaim October 7 Love Day. Officials said that they were ignorant of the fact that the inmate had been convicted of sexually molesting two boys.

• In response to a planned Ku Klux Klan visit, the county board of Walworth, Wisconsin, tried to pass a resolution opposing bigotry when someone objected to a reference to "hate groups." In a move to appease the citizen, the board passed a resolution amending the term to "unhappy groups."

A DESPERATE CRY FOR MORE DOUGHNUT BREAKS

Contract workers repairing a stretch of roadway in Pennsylvania's Schuylkill County paved over a deer carcass lying along Route 895. State transportation engineer Walter Bortree said the contractor probably just didn't see the animal, but Keither Billig, the mayor of nearby Bowmanstown, pointed out, "The deer was lying there dead for three to four weeks. You can't miss it. It's in a straightaway."

BIG DIFFERENCE

The cost of changing New York City's Department of Transportation to the Department of Infrastructure Management and Transportation was $1.4 million. That includes putting the new name on buildings, vehicles, uniforms, and stationery.

DOUBLE TROUBLE

Six months after the Dalai Lama announced confirmation of six-year-old Gedhun Choekyi Nyima as the reincarnation of the Panchen Lama, Tibetan Buddhism's second-holiest leader, the Chinese government introduced its own candidate, six-year-old Gyaincain Norbu.

Seeking to win the allegiance of Tibetans and influence the choice of the next Dalai Lama, enabling it to control Tibetan Buddhism, Beijing defended its choice as a boy with "mild manner" and "fine appearance," while denouncing the rival as a "fraud" who "violated the cardinal principles of Buddhism," including once drowning a dog.

MEET THE NEW BOSS

Within days of taking control of the capital of Afghanistan, the new Muslim Taliban government ordered every civil and military employee to grow "a proper beard" within forty-five days or be prepared for punishment. The new Department for Ordaining Good and Prohibiting Bad Deeds issued a decree on Radio Kabul that the beards must be full beards. Even trimmed beards would be reason for punishment.

PULLING A GILLIGAN

Two policemen in Chasico, Argentina, tried to demonstrate to their superiors how essential they were by faking a number of crimes, including setting off alarm bells at a school to show how quickly they could arrive on the scene, burning down part of a school, reporting robberies that didn't happen, and firing shots into their car to show proof of a shoot-out with crooks. The sudden crime wave attracted the attention of police officials, who investigated and uncovered the ruse.

THAT'S ME ON TV

Police in New Jersey's Egg Harbor Township responded to a woman's report that her boyfriend, Jerome Davis, forty, had come to her home at 10:00 P.M. and threatened her with a shotgun. He left before police arrived, but they were called back to the scene at 4:00 A.M., after the woman again called to say that Davis had come back to the house armed. She and the other occupants fled the home. When police arrived shortly after four, they cordoned off streets up to one half mile away, assigned two tactical teams armed with rifles, and evacuated surrounding houses.

Their siege drew media attention, but Davis was not in the house. Police were sure he was barricaded inside because when they arrived, they saw a light go on inside the house, but he was watching television at a relative's and saw that police had surrounded his house. For the next nine hours they attempted to talk to Davis using a bullhorn. They discovered Davis wasn't home when he called an attorney and made arrangements to turn himself in. The light had been switched on by a timer.

THE LAW'S THE LAW

A police officer in Portsmouth, Virginia, arrested two Muslim women because they were wearing veils in public. The officer reportedly thought they were in violation of a state law banning the wearing of masks in public, a law meant to apply to the Ku Klux Klan.

WRITING'S ON THE WALL

A fourth-grade teacher in Spokane, Washington, was suspended after having her class copy an obscene word that she discovered written on a table. After no one would own up to doing it, her class suggested that she take handwriting samples and have them analyzed.

PRIVILEGE OF OFFICE

Connecticut State Representative Donnie Sellers, Sr., was accused of taking a two-hundred-dollar bribe from an undercover policeman who posed as a food stamp thief in search of a gun permit. According to prosecutors, Sellers can be heard on the policeman's hidden tape recorder boasting, "I'm a politician. I ain't turning nothing down."

WHERE RUBBER MEETS THE ROAD

Washington State officials closed two highways repaired with chunks of rubber from old tires after the roads began smoking and oozing a toxic oily goo that threatened marshes on the Columbia River. In the first incident the state had used the rubber from a million old tires instead of rock or gravel to provide 7,000 cubic feet of fill when it rebuilt a 150-foot stretch of state Route 100 at the mouth of the river. Two months later asphalt pavement laid over the fill began to crack, split, and give off wisps of noxious smoke, with temperatures up to 160 degrees. In southeastern Washington, meanwhile, a 350-foot stretch of a Garfield County road began emitting smoke and even flames shortly after another repair job used chipped tires.

DON'T DO IT YOURSELF

In Norway the Buskerud County tax office billed carpenter Halvard Stensrud $1,055 for taxes on the professional services he performed as he worked on his own house. "If I'd been building the house during working hours, it may have been different," Stensrud said, "but I did everything in my free time."

FIREFIGHT

The New Jersey Department of Environmental Protection fined Robert and Sissel Juliano thirty thousand dollars for mowing down tall reeds and plants covering a vacant lot adjacent to their house. They believed they were beautifying the neighborhood. The state argued that they had destroyed vegetation growing in a designated wetland area. Their attorney pointed out that the 2.8-acre lot was periodically set ablaze by the town of Pemberton's fire department to keep the weed growth in check and that the couple had mowed the area to avoid a fire hazard. Two Superior Court judges noted that the site had been burned for seventeen years and had grown back each time and had even grown back after the Julianos' mowing. "There must be more important things the DEP can do," said one.

DREAM VS. REALITY

Despite an out-of-control crime rate and declining city services that have the District of Columbia on the verge of economic collapse, a federal planning commission spent $1.5 million to create a futuristic vision of the capital. Illustrations in a twenty-eight-page booklet that cost $60,000 to produce show futuristic flying automobiles hovering over a space age artist's rendering of the city. The plan calls for miles of freeways and bridges to be replaced and the creation of lengthy waterfront parks along the Potomac River. The booklet, *Extending the Legacy: Planning America's Capital for the 21st Century*, was the result of a five-year effort. The commission's planning, said to be looking fifty to one hundred years into the future, contradicts current plans. While it foresees tearing down the city's Southeast-Southwest Freeway, the District is about to begin spending $200 million to extend the same road. The commission also made no suggestions about how its grand designs would be funded.

MISS A TURN

Parker Brothers admitted that for the past sixty years it has misspelled Marven Gardens as "Marvin" Gardens on its popular Monopoly board game. The company said that correcting the error would be too costly.

AIN'T REALITY TOUGH ENOUGH?

• In 1995 the air force decided that its cadets no longer had to take part in an exercise in which they acted out mock rapes in a scenario that sought to instruct them in dealing with sexual assault if they were taken prisoner. Several female cadets complained that male cadets acting out the parts of the enemy forced them onto tables, removed some of their clothes, and stood between their legs. A male cadet said that his in-

structor forced him to wear a skirt and instructed
another cadet to mount him, which he did.

• At four o'clock one morning five masked gunmen invaded the Martinsville, Virginia, Memorial Hospital and entered the emergency room, took hostages,
and demanded drugs. While some employees and security guards had been warned, the doctors, nurses, and
patients in the emergency room had no idea that it was
a drill. The local police chief, also unaware of the exercise, said that it could have resulted in a shoot-out. The
hospital said that the five-minute drill was designed to
test reactions by the staff to violence. A doctor in the
emergency room called it the "most flagrant travesty of
justice, of care, of human concern that I have ever wit-
nessed in a hospital setting." Three nurses were so upset by the incident that they hired a lawyer.

• Two armed robbers burst into the offices of TCI
Cablevision of Tulsa, Oklahoma, one day in 1993, bran-
dishing handguns and screaming at employees, "Get your
[expletive] head down!" Within minutes the twenty employees were told that it was a security "seminar." Five
former employees of the office are suing TCI, charging
assault with a deadly weapon. They have already turned
down an offer of a million dollars to settle out of court.
The exercise involved real guns, shoving a guard to the
floor, and the taking of a hostage "plant" who had a gun
put to her head.

WONDERS OF FREE ENTERPRISE

• Microsoft Corporation apologized to Mexicans for a Spanish thesaurus included in its Windows 6.0 that suggests using the words *man-eater* and *savage* as alternatives for the word *Indian*. Synonyms for words such as *Western* and *lesbian* resulted in such suggestions as *Aryan, white,* and *civilized* and *pervert* and *depraved person* respectively.

• Entrusted with handling all package deliveries to the 1996 Olympics in Atlanta, United Parcel Service decided to test its own security measures by sending a fake package bomb to the Georgia World Congress Center, an Olympic events site and headquarters of the Olympics' international broadcasting facilities. The package was not detected by the internal UPS security system but instead was discovered by Olympic security guards, who assumed it was a bomb. They evacuated the center, and a bomb squad blew up the package. UPS apologized for the unnecessary evacuation of so many people, including foreign journalists headquartered there. "People don't like surprises," commented the spokesman for the State Olympic Law Enforcement Command.

WE DELIVER FOR YOU

In July 1996 the Postal Service accidentally eliminated the special ZIP code (20231) for the U.S. Patent and

Trademark Office. The mistake caused tens of thousands of patent applications to be returned marked "not deliverable." After a few days of no mail delivery the patent office inquired about the sudden dropoff. Bradford Huther, the office's associate commissioner, believed that the volume of returned applications was between 25,000 at a minimum and perhaps as high as 150,000. The Postal Service could not explain how handlers could possibly return that volume of mail for such a high-profile address. The patent office estimated that the questions of possible intellectual property losses caused by possible missed deadlines could take months to sort out.

RULES IS RULES

During bidding for wireless telephone licenses at the Federal Communications Commission, PCS 2000 L.P., a Puerto Rican company, mistakenly entered a bid of $180 million on a computerized bidding form for a license covering a market including Norfolk and Newport News, Virginia. The company had intended to bid $18 million. According to FCC rules, those who withdraw bids must pay the difference between the bid and the amount a license actually sells for. PCS asked to be excused from paying the fine. The FCC noted that the computerized bidding system gives bidders three opportunities to confirm their bids and then a chance to get a paper printout to confirm their bids again. The FCC has never granted a waiver for a penalty.

OUR
FRIENDS
THE
POLITICIANS

HUH?

New Jersey Senator Bill Bradley, commenting to reporters about possible plans to run for the presidency in 1996, said, "I'm very much now in a jazz combo, and I don't know what's going to happen next. That's the nature of what we're trying to do."

AND THEY SAID HE COULDN'T DO IT

"I am encouraged by the example of Kato Kaelin, who was relatively unknown until two weeks ago," said the former Tennessee governor and 1996 presidential hopeful Lamar Alexander, commenting on his own lack of name recognition in March 1995.

WHATEVER . . .

Oh, we didn't visit that part.

—Senator Bob Dole, departing the Rock & Roll Hall of Fame in Cleveland in June 1996. He had been asked by reporters to name his favorite rock group.

Blow in, blow out, blow off, whatever.

—Senator Bob Dole, commenting on how other Republican presidential candidates were handling the 1996 primaries.

GETTING IN TOUCH

• On the eve of the New Hampshire Republican presidential primary in 1996, Lamar Alexander was asked by a reporter at a news conference what the price was of a dozen eggs and a gallon of milk. Alexander did not respond but instead ended the press conference, then turned to an aide and said, "I need to know the price of a gallon of milk and a dozen eggs—now. I need to know right now."

• Delivering a campaign speech in Salt Lake City in 1996, Ross Perot said, "Assume that we continue to ship entire industries overseas to other countries, and then a major war breaks out 10 years from now. We go to Puerto Rico and ask them politely if they will give us medicines and pharmaceuticals for our troops who are wounded in combat. Obviously, we have to manufacture these goods within our borders to defend this great country." (Puerto Rico has been part of the United States since 1898.)

JERKUS ERECTUS

I have four years of Latin. There is no such word as homophobia. Phobia of man—homo? If they mean homosexual phobia or decadence phobia, that would be more accurate, but it is not a phobia. It may be an aversion to seeing the collapse of our society or, as Billy Graham put it, a great nation on the brink of self-destruction.

—Overly excited former congressman but then GOP presidential candidate Robert Dornan during the 1996 race.

AW, MOM!

After Ross Perot chose political economist Pat Choate to be his running mate in 1996, reporters asked Choate's mother about his chances of winning. "I don't think it will ever amount to much, but I'm proud people have that much respect for him," said Betty Choate, eighty-four. The next morning she said, "My son called me this morning and told me not to give any more interviews."

TRUER WORDS WERE NEVER SAID

I'm not trying to duck that question, but I don't want to deal with that question until this election is over.
—Senator Bob Smith of New Hampshire, when asked by a reporter about his position on term limits.

WHAT HE SAID!

For him to say, well, never mind you guys who are toiling in the vineyard that I committed to work in, I'm going to jump ship and go join hands with the political background noise that indicts you in total disregard of your personal commitment to a hard task, I think is not acceptable.
—House Majority Leader Dick Armey, criticizing a fellow member of Congress for his criticism of the House Ethics Committee.

AND YOU'RE FROM WHAT PLANET?

Former Republican Representative Fred Heineman of North Carolina, who was defeated for reelection in 1996, told the *Raleigh News and Observer* in 1995 that his congressional salary of $133,600, in addition to his annual police pension of $50,000 (he is the former police chief of Raleigh), "does not make me rich. That does not make me middle class. In my opinion that makes me lower-middle-class. When I see someone who is making anywhere from $300,000 to $750,000 a year, that's middle class. When I see anyone above that, that's upper-middle class."

3.

LIFESTYLES OF THE DUMB AND DUMBER

A Dream Is a Wish Your Heart Makes

• Jason Smallwood, twenty-six, showed up at an indoor rodeo in Bedford County, Virginia, asking to ride a bull. He admitted he had never actually ridden a bull but said he had practiced on a bucking-barrel mechanical ride before. Aboard the real thing, he lasted about three seconds when the bull threw him, trampled him, and tossed him against a fence, killing him. "He said he wanted to try it once," Todd Wood, a friend, noted. "He always wanted to try something once."

• Jeff Summers, thirty-one, of Twins Falls, Idaho, was seriously injured after he parachuted from the roof of Seattle's seventy-six-story Columbia Seafirst Center. A gust of wind collapsed his chute and blew him into the side of the building, causing him to break a window on the seventeenth floor before plummeting to a fifth-floor roof tier. Police Officer Sean O'Donnell said that according to two companions, Summers was leaving for a medical residency in Honolulu "and apparently he had always wanted to jump off the building."

SPRINGTIME FOR HITLER

French sports minister Guy Drut ordered his country's
Olympic synchronized swimming team to drop any ref-
erences to the Holocaust in a four-minute routine
planned for the Summer Games in Atlanta. Set to music
from Steven Spielberg's movie *Schindler's List*, the
routine reenacted the arrival of Jewish women in the
German death camps, the selection by Nazi doctors,
and their final march to the gas chambers, performed
by swimmers wearing black bathing suits who were to
goose-step to the side of the pool before plunging in.

ANOTHER CASE FOR *THE X-FILES*

Astronomers at Australia's Parkes Observatory were
hopeful they had made contact with intelligent life
elsewhere in the universe after their radio telescope
began picking up a distinctive radio signal every evening about dinnertime. They later discovered the signal
was coming from their microwave oven downstairs.

FORE PLAY

When a student pilot and his instructor experienced
engine trouble over Boca Raton, Florida, they lined up
for an emergency landing on the first fairway of the
municipal golf course. Four golfers remained on the

fairway, however, forcing the Piper Aero to veer off into a tree. "Everything would have been OK if those damned golfers would have moved out of the way," instructor Scott Slinko complained. "We were coming down, and they weren't moving, so I went for the tree."

The foursome insisted they never noticed the plane. "Concentration, that's the name of the game," Irv Brown, one of the golfers, explained. "We were concentrating."

ARTISTIC COMPROMISE

During the shooting of her movie *Stealing Beauty*, actress Liv Tyler, whose character was supposed to be posing for an artist, refused to bare both breasts, telling director Bernardo Bertolucci it would be "exploitative nudity." She insisted she would reveal only one breast.

THE CARNIVAL IS OVER

São Paulo cardiovascular surgeon Roberto Tullii announced that stress, caused by Brazil's poor economy, accounts for the sexual problems of sixty percent of men seeking his services. What's more, that's twice the number from ten years ago. His patients' average age also has fallen to thirty-seven from forty-seven in 1986, when Brazil began a series of austere, anti-inflation programs. Tullii told *Estado de São Paulo* that professional males are most at risk from stress-related sexual problems, explaining, "It would be hard to find a shoe-shiner suffering from impotence."

You've Come a Long Way, Baby

Germany's liberal, mostly male Free Democrats launched an equal rights campaign to open the army to women, attacking the legal exclusion of women in combat as the country's last sexist job ban. Their female counterparts rejected the call to arms, however, charging the men with raising the equal rights banner only to keep troop strength up because the number of men entering the armed forces had fallen.

Lights Out

The world's first commercial wave-powered electric generator was towed to a site off northern Scotland as the initial step in harnessing the power of the seas for cheap, clean, and renewable energy. Allan Thomson, managing director of Applied Research and Technology of Inverness, which developed the structure to convert waves into electrical energy said it would produce enough electricity to supply about two thousand homes. Less than a month later it sank.

ARTISTIC LICENSE

• When a high-tech Civil War display at Stone Mountain, Georgia, was unveiled, it featured a blue-eyed Robert E. Lee. The Confederate army general's eyes were actually brown.

• Baltimore artist Susan Luery said she carefully researched details of Babe Ruth's appearance before creating her nine-foot, eight-hundred-pound bronze statue of the baseball player for the north entrance to Oriole Park at Camden Yards. The statue, which depicts the Babe when he was a pitcher for the International League Orioles in 1914, shows him leaning on a bat and clutching a right-handed fielder's glove. Ruth was actually left-handed.

WEIGHTY MATTERS

Caterers at Barcelona's European Congress on Obesity, which brought together thirteen hundred authorities on nutrition and related consumer groups to analyze scientific information on weight, served the group typical Spanish conference fare at coffee breaks and receptions: sweet pastries, fried dough, and greasy sausages. "It's criminal," one member of an obesity association complained to the news agency Reuters while eating a sugary croissant. "They have no idea what we're struggling against."

New Age Kosher

An Israeli communications satellite launched into space was designed to follow Jewish law by not operating on the Sabbath and holy days. The Itim news agency reported that religiously observant scientists who helped plan the Amos satellite insisted that its main motor rest on the days specified in the Bible. Yigal Banat, head of the trajectory monitoring team, noted that the satellite's launch on a Friday just before the Feast of Weeks holiday made the observance particularly difficult; nevertheless, "the management of the Amos program decided to abide by this constraint in order not to break the Sabbath in Israel."

Long on Courage, Short on Foresight

When fourteen-year-old Subaru Takahashi set off from Japan in a thirty-foot yacht to try to become the youngest person to cross the Pacific Ocean alone, he told the *Mainichi Shimbun* newspaper that to help him pass the time during his two-month journey he was taking along a portable CD player but only a dozen CDs.

Is That a Baton or Are You Just Glad to See Me?

Prehistoric artifacts generally identified as tools were actually sex toys, according to British archaeologist

Timothy Taylor. Objects carved as phalluses, widely found in Upper Paleolithic art, have been prudishly interpreted as spear straighteners or batons, Taylor said, pointing out that these so-called batons "fall within the size range of dildos." He suggested they have been mistakenly identified as ritual objects because of "a modern belief that pre-modern sex was essentially a reproductive activity, and that if it wasn't, it ought to have been."

BELLING THE CAT

Scientists studying the migration routes of penguins in the Antarctic decided the best way to tell the look-alike birds apart would be to glue to their beaks bar codes like those used on supermarket packages. According to John Croxall, a biologist with the British Antarctic Survey, scanners to read the bar codes could be placed along regularly traveled penguin paths.

VEGETABLE KINGDOM

In the Thai village of Ban Huai Thaak all the adults have become addicted to an amphetamine called ya ba, according to Bangkok's *Nation* newspaper. As a result, they have begun frantically cutting down trees inside a forest reserve and selling them to pay for their habit.

Officials noted the area around the village has the highest deforestation rate in the country.

Fun and Games in China

• When a lack of snow threatened skiing competitions at the Asian Winter Games in Yabuli, Manchuria, local farmers gathered snow from valleys and mountains, put it in plastic bags, and delivered it on their backs so that the games could begin on schedule, according to the *Los Angeles Times*. "It was very difficult to find the snow," said one volunteer. "Sometimes you had to go deep in the woods."

• China announced it had invested $2.4 million to open tourism facilities for the Shennongjia region in central Hubei Province, home of the fabled Abominable Snowman. In addition to opening a park and museum dedicated to the yeti, the government began promoting the area to Chinese and foreign travel agencies. Despite years of searching for the elusive creature, the only indications that it exists are thousands of giant footprints and reddish brown hairs collected by some villagers.

TAKE THE HINT

Twice in three months Charlie Tomlinson's obituary appeared in Virginia's *Roanoke Times*. The newspaper explained that the error occurred because its employees misinterpreted a fax from Tomlinson, director of the Tomlinson Funeral Home, announcing someone else's funeral and inserted Tomlinson's name as the deceased.

OFFICIAL IDEAS

French engineer Yves Lecoffre proposed easing air pollution in Paris by installing seventy thousand fans around the city to blow away car exhaust fumes. Lecoffre, who said the fans could be placed on balconies and windowsills, estimated the project would cost less than eighty million dollars.

CELEBRITY CORNER

Actor Charlie Sheen, hoping to catch a ball, paid five thousand dollars to buy all the seats in one section behind the left-field fence at Anaheim Stadium for the first California Angels home game this season. "Anybody can catch a foul ball. I want to catch a fair ball," he said, explaining, "I didn't want to crawl over the paying public. I wanted to avoid the violence."

He sat with three friends on an aisle about twenty rows back, pounding a glove in anticipation. The Angels won, 4–3, but no ball was hit anywhere near Sheen.

PERILS OF PROSPERITY

At Bangladesh's first national conference of muggers the association representing the criminals declared that the city of Dacca was prosperous enough to support a doubling of its daily muggings, from 60 to 120. The hundred or so muggers who attended the confab took time out to acclaim their leader, Mohammad Rippon, for pulling off a record 21 attacks in just two hours.

BREWING UP TROUBLE

The LEP Collider, a seventeen-mile ring under the Franco-Swiss border where subatomic particles are smashed together at close to the speed of light, was brought to an abrupt halt in 1996. According to the European Laboratory for Particle Physics (CERN), after scientists spent five days trying to get it restarted, a team entered the accelerator and found the problem: Someone had left two empty beer bottles in a vacuum chamber.

FLUSHED WITH SUCCESS

• China's Museum of the Chinese Revolution staged the country's first exhibition of public toilets, featuring twelve hundred photos, paintings, and displays that portray China's five thousand years of toilet history. "Many foreigners who come to China leave with a very deep impression of Chinese toilets," said the exhibition's organizer, Lou Xiaoqi. "They say China doesn't care about toilets, but it's not true."

• Further evidence to that effect comes from Shanghai, where only sixty percent of the residents have indoor plumbing and the rest use chamber pots that have to be emptied and cleaned daily. The city government invested nearly a million dollars to build public toilets that resemble European villas, glitzy bars, even office buildings. The *Los Angeles Times* reported that a newly redecorated three-story public washroom on Nanyang Street was voted China's "Best Public Toilet." It features a mosaic-tiled entryway, wheelchair ramp, automatic hand dryer, air conditioning, and conference room with leather couches and a large-screen video-karaoke player. "We care about toilet culture," said Cui Yuzhen, forty-seven, deputy director of the Jing An District Sanitation Department, who vowed, "by 2000 we will have ended the era of the chamber pot."

• Some five hundred delegates attended an international toilet symposium in Hong Kong that covered such topics as design of public toilets, culture and social habits of toilet use, and environmentally friendly,

or "green," toilets. Also part of the three-day conference, according to the *Washington Post*, was this announcement by the Japan Toilet Association, which
two years earlier held the first such international toilet
symposium and claimed to have raised public awareness of toilets in Japan: "Now we have just started to
build the international toilet network. We hope the toilet network will spread over the world."

• British Scrabble player Michael Goldman, sixty-
two, filed a lawsuit against the Association of Premier
Scrabble Players for not allowing him sufficient time to
go to the bathroom during a tournament at the Burstin
Hotel in Folkestone. Goldman said he had to negotiate
five crowded hotel conference rooms, including one
crowded with a convention of cowhands, then wait in
line to use the facilities. He said he was away no more
than seven minutes, but in his absence his opponent
completed his turn and officials started Goldman's
game clock, causing him to lose four minutes of playing time, the tournament, and, ultimately, $318 in prize
money. "This may appear to be a relatively trivial matter, but it is not," Goldman's lawyer, Michael Duggan,
said, noting that Scrabble is Goldman's "recreation and
an important part of his life."

DENNIS RODMAN IS IN THE HOUSE

Women commuters in Teheran beat up an Iranian man
who rode on a bus dressed as a woman to win a thirty-

three-dollar bet with his father. The newspaper *Ette-laat* reported that the thirty-one-year-old man, identi-fied only as Mohsen, rode in the segregated female rear section of the bus, but his large body and shoes gave him away. After the women had beaten him up, a court added to his woes by sentencing him to twenty lashes for committing "an ugly and improper" act.

FREE AT LAST

In Tasmania just-widowed Stella Serth was fined three hundred dollars for disorderly conduct because she danced on her husband's grave while singing "Who's Sorry Now."

THAT OLD BLACK MAGIC

• Special precautions were taken at Cairo Inter-national Airport for two men being extradited to Qatar. The suspects, Siddiq Adam el Haji, fifty-two, and Ahmed Adam Ali, forty-eight, were accused of being master sorcerers who used black magic to obtain thirty million dollars from Qatari businessmen. Egypt's Mid-dle East News Agency reported Qatari security men in-sisted the suspects be blindfolded before boarding the flight because they feared the pair would "throw a spell" on the plane.

• In Italy, Tuscan watchmaker Fabrizio Caselli introduced a special coffin for people who fear they'll be buried prematurely. The forty-five-hundred-dollar casket is equipped with a two-way microphone-speaker, a flashlight, a small oxygen tank, a heart stimulator, and a beeper to alert an aboveground monitoring station. Caselli said that if sales meet his expectations, Italy will need to staff as many as three such emergency centers to respond to premature burial alerts.

If You're Not Part of the Solution, You're Part of the Problem

• The nation's seven soft drink vending machine makers agreed to post warning labels on 1.7 million machines, the U.S. Consumer Product Safety Commission announced. "Do not rock or tilt," the labels warn. "May cause serious injury or death. Machine will not dispense free product if tipped." The CPSC sought voluntary labeling because at least 37 people have been killed and 113 injured in soda machine accidents since 1978. The vending machine industry, which acceded to CPSC's voluntary labeling campaign to avoid government regulation, denied there is a problem, noting that the vending machines, weighing up to a ton, almost never fall over without human help, someone trying to steal money, get a free drink, or beat up a machine that took the money but gave nothing in return. "If a person's going to tip it over," Larry Eils, director of health and safety for the National Automatic Merchandising Association, "no warning label is going to stop them."

• Auto insurers announced the elimination of discounts for cars equipped with antilock brakes after concluding the safety devices do not significantly reduce accidents. The problem isn't so much the brakes themselves as it is human nature defeating technology. Drivers, who were taught to pump brakes to avoid skidding, continue to pump antilock brakes, although they shouldn't, thereby increasing stopping distances. Other people drive faster and take more risks because they believe that antilock brakes will stop them sooner, according to insurers. The move to end discounts angered some auto industry officials, who noted that the only reason they adopted the antilock technology in the first place was that insurance companies had urged them to do so.

NO MORE MONKEY BUSINESS

Brazil's environmental protection institute announced it would seek a ban against television commercials for beer and soft drinks in which chimpanzees drive and drink with bikini-clad women. Lilian Daher, spokesperson for the government agency, explained, "Driving a car and drinking beer or soda is not a monkey's natural habitat."

GAY NINETIES

Rather than let gay high school students form a club, the Salt Lake City school board voted to ban all nonacademic organizations in the city's three area high schools. The move affected some thirty service, ethnic, and sports clubs. "Everyone suffers because of the gays," complained Brett Shields, sixteen, a member of East High's Beef Club, which the Associated Press reported met "to eat steaks and burgers and attend a 'monster truck' rally."

SOME YAM

Vo Nhu Da, a farmer in central Vietnam, was forced to lock himself in his house with a 187-pound sweet potato, Hanoi's *Lao Dong* newspaper reported, after neighbors heard about the giant tuber and "came thousands of times to Da's house for a look."

LOSING ATTITUDE

Norway's Justice for Losers Association, formed in 1993, saw its profile rise three years later, when King Harald met with its founder, Ola Odegaard. Oslo's *Dagbladet* newspaper reported that 9,115 losers had registered with the organization, which receives about forty thousand dollars a year in government support.

SUSPICION CONFIRMED

Since the use of computers has become widespread in the United States, the rate of productivity growth has mysteriously plummeted, according to the *San Francisco Chronicle*, which reported experts' opinions that computers may actually be costing companies tens of billions of dollars a year. A 1992 study by SBT Accounting Systems of Sausalito, California, estimated that PC users waste five billion hours a year, worth a hundred billion dollars to the U.S. economy, waiting for programs to run, calling technical support, checking computer output for accuracy and proper formatting, helping co-workers use their applications, and organizing cluttered disk storage. The Gartner Group Inc., a research firm in Stamford, Connecticut, estimated that businesses lose twenty-six million hours of employee time each year to on-the-job game playing. Peter Sassone, an economist at Georgia Tech University, found that large companies frequently use computers to shift the burden of petty tasks from cheap clerical help to highly paid executives. As a result, managers spend less time doing managerial work, causing a staggering loss of productivity. In addition, because computers depreciate incredibly fast as new models render old ones obsolete, companies are constantly buying new, more powerful machines and software.

MUSIC LOVERS

• Officials in Vilnius, Lithuania, erected a monument to rock star Frank Zappa, explaining that even though the two had no connection, they were sure he would have visited Vilnius had he not died two years earlier.

• American scientist Dr. Hector Corona reported that dolphins sing along to the radio. By slowing down recordings of dolphins to one-quarter speed, he said he discovered that their sounds are popular hits from the likes of Mariah Carey and Bryan Adams, which they hear by picking up sound waves from radios on boats and beaches.

VEILED THREAT

The government of Kenya announced that Muslim women would have to be photographed without their veils for new national identity cards. When the women protested, the government relented and said they could have their pictures taken wearing veils.

MILES OF SMILES

Yu Qian, a dentist in China's Heilongjiang province, built an eight-foot-high tower out of twenty-eight thousand decayed teeth to promote awareness of dental hygiene.

Just Don't Make It an Olympic Event

Nearly six hundred delegates from seventeen nations gathered in the capital of the western Indian state of Goa for the first World Conference on Auto-Urine Therapy. The therapy involves drinking one's own urine. G. K. Thakkar, president of the event's host, the Water of Life Foundation, said drinking urine cured him of dysentery and eczema and made him a "bold orator." Actress Sarah Miles also insisted the practice improves her health. "I once thought it was a strange practice," said retired Admiral L. Ramadas, former chief of India's navy. "But it gives me and my wife tremendous energy and stamina."

Beat the Reaper

• In announcing approval of a prescription nasal spray to help hard-core smokers quit by delivering a half milligram of nicotine—the amount in a typical low-tar cigarette—per squirt, the Food and Drug Administration warned that smokers could become as dependent on the nicotine in the spray as they are on cigarettes.

• The FDA also approved a machine that filters fat from patients who cannot be helped by low-fat diets or drugs. The Liposorber works much the way dialysis removes toxins from a kidney patient's body: by removing blood from the patient's body, filtering out cholesterol, then returning the filtered blood to the patient. The FDA warned the machine is not a cure since cholesterol levels creep back up within fourteen days, requiring patients to undergo the treatment every two or three weeks indefinitely at between fifteen hundred and two thousand dollars a treatment.

Money Talks

Thirty-five percent of Americans surveyed in a poll reported in the *New Republic* said they would favor printing ads on dollar bills if doing so would result in lower taxes.

Shirking-Class Heroes

A Transylvanian mayor, Gheorghe Funar, proposed making the handles of shovels of city workers too short to lean on so the workers will get on with their work.

Cure for a Cookout

A federal court in Cleveland ordered the destruction of sixteen thousand Stimulator devices being marketed as a medical product without the required approval of the Food and Drug Administration. The Stimulator, endorsed by daredevil Evel Knievel and sold for $79.80 plus shipping, is advertised as alleviating pain and medical ailments, but, according to Assistant U.S. Attorney Alex Rokakis, "the FDA has determined the device is a gas-grill igniter."

IS THAT A PYTHON IN YOUR POCKET— OR ARE YOU GLAD TO SEE ME?

The Society for the Prevention of Cruelty to Animals requested that the Malaysian news media carry "positive reports" about pythons. The group complained that after news of a twenty-three-foot python killing and trying to swallow a twenty-nine-year-old rubber plantation worker in Johore State, Malaysians began indiscriminately killing any snakes they encountered.

OVERORGANIZED CRIME

Ukrainian bandits who menace travelers in eastern Hungary began issuing receipts to victims to show any rival gangs they might subsequently encounter. *The European* reported the documents certify that the victims have nothing of value left to steal.

ALL QUIET ON THE EASTERN FRONT

The Associated Press reported that although the Bosnians have their own currency, called the dinar, they prefer to do business in deutsche marks, saving their own currency for small change. For small purchases, many Bosnian merchants don't even bother with change. Instead they hand out Bosnian bubble gum, which comes with a color photo of a topless woman.

THE WORLD'S A STAGE

Hollywood producer Murray Siegel announced he was starting a business to help entertainers who want to testify at congressional hearings. For twenty thousand dollars, his firm would develop informational packets in language that the stars can understand, arrange appointments with members of Congress and political leaders, schedule testimony before subcommittees, and provide an entourage. "We're trying to create a scenario," Siegel told *Roll Call*, "where the voice of a celebrity can move a nation."

THAT'S ALL, FOLKS

• Two years in a row Canadian Football League teams drafted dead players. In 1995, during a special draft of players from a defunct Las Vegas team, the Ottawa Rough Riders selected defensive end Derrell Robertson, who had died following an auto accident nearly five months earlier. "I don't know how it happened," Rough Riders coach Jim Gilstrap said. "The league didn't know until we told them. And we didn't know until a week ago, when we couldn't find him."

The next year the league's Montreal Alouettes selected James Eggink of Northern Illinois University in the college draft, only to learn a few hours later that he had died three months before. "I'm not making excuses," Alouettes owner Jim Speros said, noting the draft list had 560 names and "the research process can be very difficult."

• Two guests at a wedding in Copenhagen, Denmark, died and nine others were wounded when a thirty-six-year-old Turkish immigrant at the festivities celebrated according to his custom by drawing a pistol and firing twelve shots into the air. Unfortunately he had overlooked the fact that the celebration was indoors. The bullets ricocheted off the concrete ceiling and struck the victims.

THE AMERICAN WAY

Pointing out that "not everyone thinks airline food is a joke," American Airlines said its reservation clerks were flooded with calls from people seeking copies of its new cookbook, which tells how to re-create the "subtle flavors and tantalizing aromas" of airline cuisine in their own kitchens. "Because some of our customers frequently request recipes so they can prepare their in-flight favorites at home, we asked our executive chefs to adapt a few of these new recipes" for smaller portions, according to the Preface to the airline's eighteen-page booklet of recipes, *A Taste of Something Special.*

PROGRESS, SCHMOGRESS

Several ultra-Orthodox rabbis in Israel banned the use of a "purity computer" to determine when people may have sex. The hand-held device helps couples comply with Jewish law, which forbids sex from twelve hours before menstruation starts to seven days after it ends. Instead of turning to rabbis for help with the calculation, the woman need only enter information about her menstrual cycle to learn when sex is permissible. Rabbi Yosef Halevi Eliashiv, an authority on Jewish law, warned that the "purity computer" might just be the start of technology's taking over rabbis' traditional authority.

WEIGHTY MATTERS

Nutrition labels on food might actually be making people's diets worse, according to Purdue University researcher Richard Mattes. As part of a project to show that what people know about food determines how much they eat, Mattes found that when subjects were told that the lunch he served them was low in fat, they ate more during the rest of the day than subjects who were told that the lunch contained normal levels of fat. Both groups received the same lunch. "There's no question," Matte concluded, that people who choose low-fat foods some of the time overcompensate by eating too much at other times.

LACK OF GRATITUDE

In Spokane, Washington, Michael and Diane Moore filed a lawsuit against the Nine Mile Falls School District accusing middle-school teacher Joanne Bovey of forcing their daughter Kate to attend prayer sessions and religious counseling after the girl confided that she and a friend had used a Ouija board.

YOUR MONEY OR YOUR LIFE

• Kidnappers in the Philippines have become so brazen that they have begun accepting checks for ransom. According to the Movement for Restoration of Peace and Order, a crime watch organization in Manila, many of the 155 people kidnapped for ransom in 1995 paid with checks ranging from $11,500 to more than $38,000.

• *Asiaweek* magazine reported that some Philippine kidnappers now demand a ransom before abducting the victim. Others are willing to haggle over the amount. A recent case involved construction magnate Felipe Cruz, who was dining in a Manila restaurant when a man informed him he would be kidnapped sometime after dessert. When Cruz was shown other men waiting in cars outside the restaurant to abduct him, he paid—but only after negotiating the would-be kidnappers' demand down from $1.15 million to $385,000.

WHILE WAITING FOR WALLY WORLD TO REOPEN

• The World Tourism Organization and the United Nations Educational, Scientific and Cultural Organization announced plans to turn Africa's slave route into a tourist attraction. The groups would help restore sites such as forts along the Ghanaian coast.

• The Polish government hired former Sex Pistols manager Malcolm McLaren to help with a media campaign to make Warsaw trendy. He called the media campaign "a tough old gig," but told *W* magazine, "there's a fantastic energy there."

• One of Russia's most feared prisons began offering holidays for the country's nouveaux riches. Described as "recreational training of the personality," the seven-day stay at Schlisselburg Fortress, near St. Petersburg, costs $550. Guests remain locked in their cells, with short breaks, and eat only prison food. No vodka is permitted. "We will be treating people like prisoners," holiday organizer Aleksandr Nefyodov said, "although we will not be beating them."

• A group of German builders announced plans to erect part of the Berlin Wall in Broward County, Florida, as the key attraction of a theme park intended to bring South Florida "the horrors of forty years of Communist rule in East Germany." The twenty-acre thirty-million-dollar venture will include checkpoints, watchtowers, guard dogs, electrified barriers, and anti-tank emplacements. Visitors also will have the opportunity to attempt an escape across the wall. Project director Jürgen Rosskothen explained, "We want to show future generations what the reality of East Germany was."

• The militant Islamic group Party of God, or Hezbollah, linked to kidnappings and bombings in Lebanon and abroad, announced it is turning from terrorism to tourism. According to the *Washington Post*, Hezbollah leaders, eager to shore up the group's credentials as a legitimate political organization in anticipation of an eventual peace treaty between Lebanon and Israel, are cooperating with Lebanon's Tourism Ministry to attract Western visitors to the famous Roman ruins at Baalbek, now a Hezbollah stronghold. Party officials posted English-language welcome signs, helped install lighting and sound equipment amid the ruins, and generally relaxed their insistence on strict Islamic observance, which discourages the wearing of shorts and other signs of Western decadence. Noting that the Iranian-backed militants no longer see kidnappings as a political tactic, the local Hezbollah official in Baalbek told the *Post* that one European diplomat had commented, "Baalbek is safer than Oklahoma."

TRICK PHOTOGRAPHY

While television's Katie Couric and Willard Scott lauded the giant Dudley the Dragon balloon in New York's 1995 Thanksgiving Day parade, accompanying shots of the balloon that viewers saw had been video-taped weeks before during a test run. The balloon had deflated earlier along the parade route after hitting a tree, according to parade producer Jean McFadden, who decided to air the recorded material because "there is nothing as disappointing as running a blank space and saying, 'We're sorry, the balloon didn't make it.' " NBC producer Michael Morrison backed the decision, explaining the broadcast was "an entertainment special. It is not a news special, so it's not like we're duping the audience."

SPORTSMANSHIP IN THE NINETIES

• Police in Raytown, Missouri, charged James Aldridge, thirty-nine, with threatening his son's baseball coach because he didn't like the position the boy was playing. Witnesses said when the coach of the seven-year-old and eight-year-old players wouldn't heed the father's persistent requests to move his son to an infield position, Aldridge kicked off his shoes and crouched in a martial arts stance, then threatened the coach with a metal bat. Finally, police reported, he went to his car and returned with a gun tucked in his waistband.

• A bench-clearing brawl delayed a minor-league baseball game between the Winston-Salem Warthogs and Durham Bulls for thirty-two minutes. Ten players were ejected, and one was hospitalized after being knocked unconscious and losing several teeth. The donnybrook occurred on "Strike Out Domestic Violence" night.

• In upstate New York, Hamilton College president Eugene M. Tobin banned spectators from the school's hockey game against Hobart College after fans had delayed a previous game against Wesleyan University for ten minutes by littering the ice with hundreds of pieces of fruit, live mice, a dead squirrel, fish, a kielbasa, and an inflatable doll when Hamilton scored a goal. Hamilton supporters traditionally pelt the opposing goalie with tennis balls whenever their team scores the first goal in its home hockey opener. Not only did fans escalate the assault against Wesleyan, but they also added a second bombardment because Hamilton's first goal came only twelve seconds into the game. Late-arriving fans who missed it lobbed more debris onto the ice when the Continentals scored again.

HARDLY WET

Although Guy Delage, forty-two, completed a twenty-four-hundred-mile solo swim across the Atlantic, some critics wondered when he found time to swim. Outfitted with flippers, a wet suit, a high-tech kickboard, and other gear provided by sponsors, Delage spent at least fourteen hours a day on board his fifteen-foot raft cooking, sleeping, talking with his wife via radio, giving news interviews, and making observations for marine scientists. His supporters conceded that Delage made more progress at night aboard the wind-powered raft than while actually in the water. French swimmer Stefan Caron, who won a bronze medal at the 1992 Olympics, dismissed Delage's effort as little more than "bathing."

THANKS FOR NOTHING

British animal rights activist Vicki Moore, thirty-nine, was hospitalized in serious condition after being gored nine times during a bull-running festival in Coria, Spain. She was filming a documentary about how the bulls are mistreated when a half-ton bull attacked her.

FRUITFUL NEGOTIATIONS

Four kindergarten teachers upset school officials in Gastrip, Denmark, by declaring they no longer would peel the oranges that their nineteen pupils brought with them for their daily snack. Explaining that peeling oranges wasn't their job and was taking time away from their teaching, the teachers told the children who wanted to eat oranges to bring them from home already peeled. A compromise was reached when the teachers agreed to cut the unpeeled oranges into wedges.

STICKING IT TO THE BIG APPLE

New Yorkers demonstrated a willingness to pay cash for sticks and twigs at the city's open-air markets, reportedly to bring them some contact with nature. "It's getting bigger all the time," said James Stannard of the Harvester farm in Highland, New York, which sells pussy willow branches for three dollars a bunch. "When we prune trees, what we used to just throw out we bunch up and bring it to the city and sell it."

TIME WELL SPENT

Researchers at Tokyo's Keio University announced they have taught pigeons to distinguish cubist-style paintings from impressionist ones. Psychologist Shingeru

Watanabe reported the birds can correctly identify the
cubist work ninety percent of the time.

Unholy Matrimony

An Egyptian court of appeals ordered a happily married couple to divorce after declaring the husband,
Cairo University Professor Nasr Hamed Abu Zeid, had
deserted Islam. Judge Farouq Abdel Alim ruled that
Abu Zeid's academic writings made him a non-Muslim
and noted that Egyptian law forbids marriage between
a Muslim woman and non-Muslim man. Abu Zeid's
wife, fellow Professor Ibtehal Yunis, vowed to stand by
her man, although she faces imprisonment as an adul-
teress for continuing to consort with him.

Fighting for the Right to Park

In the northern Nigerian city of Kano, a fight over a
parking space escalated into ethnic riots that killed at
least five people. The trouble began when a taxi driver
and a merchant from different tribes argued about
parking in the crowded marketplace. Both called on
their tribesmen to back them up. According to police
spokesperson Abdullahi Hashimu, word of the clash
spread through the market, sparking other fights and
spilling onto city streets. People battled with sticks,

machetes, and stones and rampaged through neighborhoods, burning shops and cars and attacking houses.

THE BIGGER THEY ARE

Italian mountaineer Reinhold Messner, fifty, the first man to climb Mount Everest without an oxygen mask and tank, was injured after falling off a wall at his home in Italy. Messner's brother, Hubert, explained that the two men often climbed the walls around Messner's castle.

IDLE CHATTER

• Astronomers who use radio telescopes to probe other galaxies complained to the International Telecommunications Union that interference from cellular phones was threatening their research.

• Since Poland's post-Communist government stopped routinely tapping phone lines, Polish Telecommunications reported having trouble handling the rapidly rising number of calls from people no longer afraid to speak freely. *Zycie Warszawy* reported the utility "has been in torment over the fact that citizens do not respect what they have. They use telephone lines to convey trifling information, even gossip." The phone company recently threatened to cut off service to a popular television show, for instance, complaining "too many people were calling the program."

LAND OF THE SETTING SUN

Japan's Omrom Corporation unveiled its earthquake alarm, dubbed Shaking Boy. The device senses seismic activity, indicates its magnitude, then starts flashing an emergency beacon and announcing useful emergency procedures, such as "Dive under the table."

SCHOOL DAZE

Nearly seventy people were injured in Bangladesh when police clashed with students demanding the right to cheat on final exams. Education officials reported students used homemade bombs, field hockey sticks, and stones to attack police and examination monitors at dozens of exam centers. One teacher was hacked to death in Narail district after he tried to stop the cheating. More than eight thousand students were expelled for cheating and attacking monitors during just the first week of the monthlong testing.

MAYBE NEXT TIME
Hours before Pope John Paul II arrived for evening service at Sacred Heart Cathedral in Newark, New Jersey, during his 1995 U.S. visit, eighty elderly parishioners boarded buses for the Atlantic City casinos. Church officials said the Atlantic City trip had been planned months before the papal visit.

WAY TO GO
Drug addicts in southern India began paying to be bitten on the tongue by snakes. Drug therapist Prakhas Chandran of a therapy center in Paloarivattom warned that a bite from the unidentified snake could be deadly, but he noted that the venom is strong enough to give a bitten addict a high lasting up to sixteen hours.

MISSING THE POINT
Iranian Deputy Education Minister Hossein Herati assured critics of new classes on family planning for female high school students that they would not actually discuss sex. Instead, he said, the classes will deal only with the consequences of the population increase, not the causes.

JURY OF WHOSE PEERS?

Barbara Adams, an alternate juror at the 1996 Whitewater trial of James and Susan McDougal, was dismissed by the judge for giving a television interview to the show *American Journal*. Adams, thirty-one, attended the trial for two weeks wearing a Star Trek uniform, including a phaser and communication device on her belt. She told the interviewer that she was on a mission to spread the show's moral values of peace, tolerance, and faith in humanity.

A printshop supervisor in real life, Adams said she regularly wears the uniform to work and commands the USS Artemis, a group of "Trekkies" in Little Rock, Arkansas. After her dismissal she explained that she wore the uniform every day "for the same reason or the same way that any other officer in a military branch would wear their uniform. I'm proud of my uniform. I'm proud of what it stands for."

THE AGE OF PARANOIA

An Opinion Dynamics poll found that fifty-nine percent of Americans believe that Congress deliberately writes confusing legislation to "deceive the public."

WHEN "ART" IS JUST SHORT FOR ARTHUR

• British artist Tony Kaye arrived in San Francisco with his latest work of art: *Roger—by Tony Kaye*. "Roger" was Roger Powell, a homeless man whom Kaye displayed inside a steel-framed box. Kaye said that while appearing as a work of art, Roger "either just sits or he walks around, takes notes and is very friendly." Powell, who also appeared at galleries in London and Los Angeles, signed a contract allowing Kaye to sell him to any interested art collector.

• Vincent Gothard, twenty-five, a college senior and fine arts major at the University of Florida, was charged with animal cruelty for an art project in which he dipped forty live baby mice into resin, then cut the material into cubes. His lawyer said that the mice died instantly and that the project was "clearly artistic expression and probably protected by the First Amendment."

• Eugene Calamari, Jr., thirty-eight, a former Electrolux vacuum cleaner salesman who became a self-proclaimed performance artist, introduced an act in which he lies on the floor and lets volunteers from the audience vacuum him with an upright vacuum cleaner. Afterward he asks participants to write down their feelings. Calamari said that the idea came to him after seeing "a lot of people use each other and step on each other's rights."

• Art historian Paco Cao, who studies the relationship between art and commerce, rents his body out through a New York City nonprofit organization that sponsors public art projects. Anyone can get a Paco Cao Rent-a-Body gift certificate, enabling the recipient to do anything with him as long as it doesn't involve violence or sex. For $35 an hour Cao will act as a lifeless object. At $70 per hour he'll engage in conversation. For $150 per hour Cao provides the recipient with "total mind function."

• British artist Damien Hirst specializes in displaying sliced-up animal bodies, usually floating in formaldehyde-filled glass-walled tanks. His work titled *This Little Piggy Went to Market* consists of a large pig cut in half lengthwise. The two halves are displayed so that all internal organs are visible. Various displays of his work in New York City galleries were investigated by the city health department, which had fears about rotting cow meat. One display, featuring two dead cows hooked by a hydraulic machine to simulate a sex act between them, was eventually canceled because of health concerns.

• In 1996 the Parc de la Tête d'Or Zoo in Lyons, France, put two humans on display in an empty bear cage. The two actors, dressed in dark suits, hats, and sunglasses, spent two hours each day watching a broken television set and eating peanuts. The two, members of the theater group the Transformers, said that they were trying to reach those people who didn't usually attend the theater.

• That same year the Copenhagen Zoo placed a Danish human couple in a Plexiglas-walled apartment between the baboons and two lemurs. The zoo said that it was intended to make visitors reconsider their connection to the world of nature. The human couple, an acrobat and a writer, complained about living next to lemurs, because "exactly once every hour they mark their territory with uninhibited screaming."

TOO MUCH BOOK LEARNIN'

Canadian art student Jubal Brown, twenty-two, of the Ontario College of Art and Design announced plans to complete a personal mission to vomit on art masterpieces in primary colors. He began by throwing up blue gelatin and cake icing on Piet Mondrian's *Composition in Red, White and Blue* at the Museum of Modern Art in New York. Next he threw up in red on Raoul Dufy's *Harbour at le Havre* at the Art Gallery of Ontario. Calling the paintings stale, obedient, lifeless crusts, Brown said that his mission is to destroy art, to liberate individuals and living creatures from its banal, oppressive representation.

C STUDENTS ARISE!

Some parents in Tolland, Connecticut, decried a local school program that rewarded students for good grades as "elitist." School officials noted that since the program was put in place, the number of students on the honor roll had risen fifteen percent.

WE DON'T HUNT NO WHALES 'ROUND HERE

In Texas the Lindale Independent School District rejected thirty-two books for an advanced English class because they contained values that conflicted with the community. Among the banned books was *Moby Dick*.

DAYDREAM NATION

When a citizenship instructor gave parts of the U.S. naturalization test to seven high school history classes in Washington State, half flunked. What's more, seventy-six percent of the students didn't know how many justices serve on the Supreme Court; seventeen percent couldn't identify the country the United States fought in the Revolution; sixty percent didn't know that the president was the military commander in chief, and eighty-three percent didn't know that the Constitution is the supreme law of the land. Ninety percent of the state's immigrants routinely pass the test.

WHO'S OUR NEXT CONTESTANT, EINSTEIN?

After eleven-year-old Michael Kearney of Tennessee became the youngest boy to graduate from college, according to the *Guinness Book of Records*, he revealed that his ambition is to become a television game show host.

THE SLOW LEAK IN IOWA

Following revelations that the White House amassed FBI files on President Clinton's political opponents, the *New York Times* conducted a public opinion poll to determine the political fallout, if any, from the story. While a full seventy-five percent of the respondents said that the FBI files story had no effect on their opinion of the president, two percent said the episode actually made them "think better of" the president.

HEY, VERN, DON'T THAT MAKE YOU MAJORITY LEADER?

During the 1994 congressional elections, then House Speaker Tom Foley was in a tough race (which he eventually lost) with Republican George Nethercutt. Polling in the fall revealed that thirty percent of the voters in the city of Spokane, in the heart of Washington State's Fifth Congressional District, believed that whichever candidate won, Foley or Nethercutt, he would be the next Speaker of the House.

TEACHING SPORTSMANSHIP

A man in Albuquerque, New Mexico, was sentenced to two days in jail for sharpening a buckle on his son's football helmet. The buckle cut five players on an opposing team. The seventeen-year-old son told the judge that his father purposely sharpened the buckle because he was angry about calls by officials at his son's games.

DUMB
AROUND
THE GLOBE

MR. SCIENCE

Msweli Mdluli, a member of Swaziland's Parliament, told a public gathering that the country's continuing drought was caused by women not covering their heads. "The majority of women in the country no longer cover their heads, and this is one strong reason there has been little rain," Mdluli said. "So long as women continue to ignore culture, the drought will never go."

BUT THEY LOVED ERASERHEAD

The Shi'ite Muslim guerrilla group Hezbollah criticized the movie *Independence Day* after it opened in Beirut

as a propaganda film that championed and promoted
the "unity which Israel seeks between the 'super' Jewish mind and the growing American power to dominate
the world under the slogan of defending humanity."

WHEN IS A NAKED GUY
WITH A GUN *NOT* SCARY?

According to a report by the Defense Intelligence
Agency, one of the most prominent leaders among
Liberia's warring factions engaged in endless civil war
is "Gen. Butt Naked." As the DIA put it, "His 'nom du
guerre' probably comes from his propensity for fighting
naked. He probably believes that fighting in this manner terrorizes the enemy and brings good luck or, in
the Liberian context, good 'juju.' Belief in magic is
widespread in Liberia and accounts for some of the
outrageous behavior of Liberian fighters of all factions."

COURTESY CRAZY

July in Singapore is National Courtesy Month, an annual event since 1979. Past campaigns involved ads and
banners instructing people to behave overseas, to be
on time, to let others off of public transportation first,
and not to overload their plates at buffet tables. The
1996 campaign slogan was "Courtesy—that's my kind
of world."

DID THEY FLY IN?

Tramps from across the globe met in the port city of Mar del Plata, Argentina, in 1996 to hold a summit meeting. According to the founder of the Free Tramps Movement, Pedro Ribeira, fifty-seven, topics on the agenda included "the liberation of man from materialism" and "cheap eating on the road."

THE ETERNAL TRADE-OFF: LOW CRIME OR TOOTH DECAY?

About 600 million Chinese citizens do not brush their teeth, according to the *Xinmin Evening News*, and about 1.2 billion buy fewer than two tubes of toothpaste annually.

MAYBE WE WORRY TOO MUCH

Thailand's Deputy Interior Minister, Pairoj Lohsoonthorn, told officials of the Land Department to take bribes because it "is considered a part of traditional Thai culture." He suggested taking bribes of any amount, with the only stipulations being not to ask for bribes up front and not to set specific prices.

YOU MAY ALREADY BE A WINNER

After undergoing surgery to remove a lump of cholesterol from a neck artery, Philippine President Fidel
Ramos announced he would auction off the lump to
raise money to help the poor. "I'm preserving a relic
here which I will use for fund-raising for a worthy pur-
pose," he said.

PEOPLE WHO NEED TO WATCH MORE TV

In Spain hundreds of terrified television viewers flooded
radio and television stations with telephone calls one
weekend after the Telecinco network broadcast news
flashes of alien spaceships hovering over New York City.
The "flashes" were part of a promotion for the film *Independence Day*, which was about to open in Spain. The
panic ensued despite a text message on the screen warning that it was only an advertisement.

THE ROSS PEROT OF RIO

Rio de Janeiro mourned the death of the famous chim-
panzee Tiao, who passed away in 1996 less than a
month short of his thirty-fourth birthday. The chimp, a
favorite attraction at the Rio Zoo, ran for mayor in 1988
as the candidate of the Brazilian Banana party, which
sought to use him as a protest vote. Tiao came in third,

with four hundred thousand votes. At his death the mayor declared an eight-day mourning period and flags at the zoo were flown at half-staff.

LIFE IN THE OTHER SUPERPOWER

After a drinking binge with Chechen separatist rebels, a group of Russian soldiers from the 106th Motor Rifle Division sold their opponents a tank and an armored combat vehicle for six thousand dollars.

WIDE WORLD OF SPORTS

• Transylvania's Stefan Sigmond, twenty-nine, got into the record books again in 1996 by smoking 800 cigarettes in under six minutes, breaking his 1995 record of 750 cigarettes. He had mounted the cigarettes on a cylinder, so that he could smoke them all at once. "I am a little bit dizzy and I have a headache and an awful taste in my mouth but I am sure everything will pass away," he said afterward. Also in 1995, Stefan had eaten twenty-nine boiled eggs in four minutes.

• Two teenage construction workers in China decided on a bet to see who could smoke the most cigarettes, the loser paying for all the tobacco used. The first smoker, identified by the *Jin Wan Bao* newspaper of Tianjin only as Liu, gave in after smoking forty cigarettes. His friend Wu, egged on by a gathering crowd, continued smoking, at a rate of up to five at once, until he had smoked a hundred cigarettes. He then collapsed and died.

4.

DUMB AS CHARGED

POOR TIMING

Brian Witham, twenty-five, and James Lertola, twenty, broke out of the Marble Valley Prison near Rutland, Vermont, just before federal authorities unexpectedly arrived at the prison to deliver a warrant charging Witham with a series of armed robberies in several New England states. So instead of the Vermont corrections department sending out routine wanted flyers to New England police departments, the two fugitives activated a net of local, state, and federal police that stretched from Bangor to New York, according to Bureau of Alcohol, Tobacco, and Firearms spokesperson William Pickett, who noted, "We launched an incredibly intensive investigation."

Meanwhile the two fugitives were sitting in a stolen car in Dartmouth, Massachusetts, when a police officer approached them. They ran into the woods but left behind a list of things to do: "Drive to Maine, get safer place to stay, buy guns, get Marie, get car—Dartmouth, do robbery, go to New York." Agents staking out the Port Authority bus terminal in Manhattan spotted Lertola shortly after the Maine to New York bus arrived. Once he was apprehended, he told them where to find Witham.

IT HAD TO BE EWE

Police in Palmerston North, New Zealand, arrested Shane Patrick Neho, seventeen, and a younger accomplice for breaking into Barbarella's sex shop. The suspects fled with a blow-up woman, a female mannequin dressed in rubber underwear, a large drinking mug shaped like a vagina, and an inflatable sheep. "We have not yet ascertained why a sex shop should be stocking blow-up sheep," Sergeant Ollie Outrim told the *New Zealand Herald*, "especially as Palmerston North has a large sheep population."

THE NAME GAME

• After his latest arrest in San Rafael, California, oft-convicted flasher Ubiquitous Perpetuity God, sixty-eight, disclosed that he changed his name to give his victims "some type of awareness of God."

• Dallas police arrested an eighteen-year-old Roadway Express loading dock worker who tried to cash a check made out to his employer by presenting a photo ID as proof that he was indeed "Roadway V. Express." The Western Union clerk told the man, "OK, Mr. Express, I'll be right back," explaining he had to get the money from another room, where he called police.

BARE ESSENTIALS

After being convicted of fraud in Kansas City, Kansas, Thomas Wayne Whitlow appeared at his sentencing hearing wearing only shackles and a white sheet guards wrapped around him after he demanded to attend the hearing naked. "He told me he was mad at everyone," his lawyer, Barry Albin, said. "They asked me what to do, and I said bring him in naked, and that's what they did." U.S. District Judge Kathryn H. Vratil didn't object to Whitlow's appearance.

CREDIT WHERE IT'S DUE

Convicted murderers John Sosnovske, forty-two, and Laverne Pavlinac, sixty-two, served four years of their life sentences before they were released when the real killer confessed. The Oregon couple had been convicted in the first place because Pavlinac confessed to killing twenty-three-year-old Taujna Bennett and implicated Sosnovske. Even though at her trial Pavlinac admitted making up the whole story because she was trying to escape an abusive relationship with Sosnovske, the jury believed her original taped confession. Sosnovske had no choice but to plead no contest in order to avoid the death penalty.

Four years later Keith Hunter Jesperson insisted that he was the one who had killed Bennett. He also admitted killing seven other women, earning the epithet

"Happy-Face Killer" for drawing a smiling face on letters he sent to the news media taking credit for the crimes.

VEHICULAR MISHAPS

• Donald Sprague, twenty-four, called Superior Court Judge Robert Neustadter to say that he would be unable to attend his scheduled sentencing for car theft in Mays Landing, New Jersey, because his own car had been stolen. "He would have been sentenced but for the fact that he was the victim of his own crime," prosecutor Joel Mayer said. "It's too funny."

• A hatchet-wielding man who held up a gas station in Bradenton, Florida, made off with three hundred dollars but forgot to fill up his tank. Police arrested Jeffrey Alan McLeod, twenty-nine, after a brief high-speed chase when his car sputtered to a stop.

• A man who was shooting at vehicles on interstate highways in Kansas City, Kansas, made the mistake of firing a bullet that hit the side door of an unmarked police van driven by crime scene investigators Gary McIntosh and James Locke. "It missed both of us by inches. Pieces of the bullet ended up beneath our seats, in between us," said McIntosh, whose call for backup led to the arrest of Michael Regan, twenty-two.

New Theories of Relativity

Authorities in Pawtucket, Rhode Island, charged Mario Garcia, thirty-one, with assault after he punctured his mother-in-law's esophagus by jamming two eight-inch steel crucifixes down her throat during an exorcism. Garcia's wife, father-in-law, brother-in-law, and three children had gathered around the forty-seven-year-old woman while he attempted to chase a demon from her. "I've seen suspects who thought they had psychic powers," police captain John Haberle said, "but never one that had a family who believed it, too."

Attention Shoppers

Colorado Springs, Colorado, police investigating a bank robbery arrested Ricky Lee Pitts, thirty-four, after bank employees followed the suspect from the bank across a parking lot and into a Kmart. A clerk said the suspect asked directions to the men's clothing section, bragging "he had a lot of money and wanted to buy some new clothes."

Practice Makes Perfect

After two weeks in the women's cellblock of Norway's Stavanger District Jail, a thirty-year-old Peruvian prisoner arrested with a false passport notified prison guards that "she" was really a man. According to Oslo's *Verdens Gang* newspaper, the prisoner, who was arrested wearing heavy makeup and women's clothing, was assigned to the women's cellblock after a body search at the airport and a strip search at the jail. "It seems pretty clear," police inspector Leif Ole Topnes said, "that our body search techniques aren't good enough."

SHORT FUSE, BIG BANG

• Just before he was executed in Texas for stabbing a man to death, John Fearance, Jr., forty, called the incident "a bad psychotic break." He explained that he snapped and went on a rampage that led to the murder after returning home from his job at a car repair shop and finding that his wife had baked him a casserole with meat. He said he liked his meat separate.

• Police who charged Framingham, Massachusetts, insurance executive Richard Rosenthal, forty, with murdering his wife by slitting her from her throat to her navel and impaling her heart and lungs on a stake said he told them that she had criticized him for burning their pasta dinner. "I had an argument," he explained. "I overcooked the ziti."

• In England, Elaine Simpson was sentenced to four years in prison after she admitted killing her husband, Charles, because he couldn't stand the time she spent on the telephone. When he finally hid the phone from her, she stormed out of the home, then returned two days later and stabbed him with a kitchen knife.

Till Death Do Us Part

Authorities in Pemberton Township, New Jersey, accused Forrest D. Fuller, twenty-eight, of murdering his girlfriend, then taking her corpse to West Virginia with the intention of marrying it. Just after crossing the Pennsylvania–West Virginia state line, Fuller reportedly stopped at a tavern and tried to strike up a conversation with the barmaid by telling her that his dead girlfriend was outside in the car. After he showed her and a man working at the bar the body of Jodie Myers, twenty, in the backseat, sheriff's deputies arrested him. They also found a wedding dress in Fuller's trunk.

Seemed Like a Good Idea at the Time

A bicyclist who confronted three well-dressed men walking to their hotel in Alexandria, Virginia, pointed what looked like a 9mm semiautomatic handgun at them and demanded money. The three men turned out to be off-duty federal agents, who drew their own weapons and fired more than twenty shots, hitting the would-be robber, as well as three cars, a truck, two houses, and an office building. The injured suspect's weapon turned out to be a pellet gun.

THE CRIMINAL MIND

• Michael Myers, a bank robber in Ontario, Canada, handed a teller a note demanding fifty- and one-hundred-dollar bills or he would blow up the bank. The note was written on a bank withdrawal ticket that also featured his name and signature. He was sentenced to two years in jail.

• Police in Trenton, New Jersey, had little trouble apprehending Crawford ("Sonny") Brownlee after he robbed the Trenton Savings Bank of $1,300. Brownlee fled the bank but stopped just a couple blocks away at Mama's Chicken to order the special: a bag of thirty-four chicken wings for $5.75. The coowner of Mama's noticed that the man was sweating heavily and that he had first ordered the chicken to eat there, then quickly changed it to a takeout order. He alerted police, who found Brownlee on the street a short time later.

• A Long Island cat burglar tried to steal a five-hundred-pound safe from the second floor of a building by dragging it down the steps. He lost his balance and fell down fourteen steps, followed by the safe, which landed on him and killed him. The safe was empty.

• When two men tried to rob the Norwegian postal service's cash transport between the northern towns of Bodø and Narvik, they were surprised by thirty heavily armed police, a helicopter, and a fleet of police cars waiting for them. Authorities explained the pair, Swedes in their mid-thirties, had drawn up careful plans for the robbery but lost them. Police found the plans in an unclaimed suitcase left at Oslo's Fornebu Airport, then kept tabs on the men for nearly six months, waiting for them to strike.

• Police in Evansville, Indiana, said that Gary Brewer, thirty-five, went into the Apollo Liquor Store and ordered a bottle of wine, presenting his driver's license to a clerk, as required by state law. He then demanded cash, knocked the clerk down, and fled the scene on a bicycle with a hundred dollars. Police quickly caught up with him because he left the license at the store.

• Police in Pennsauken, Pennsylvania, quickly tracked down and arrested the chief suspect in the robbery of a business because they discovered that the thief had held the establishment's door open with a traffic ticket while he looted the place. When he fled, he left the ticket, bearing his name and address, stuck in the door for police to find.

• Rudard N. Phillips applied for a welding job at Graterford Prison in Pennsylvania. Prison officials running a standard background check quickly found the man's twenty-seven-year-long criminal record and the fact that he was then currently wanted for a parole violation in Florida. He was soon arrested.

• Two neighbors took a Maryland State Police cruiser for a joyride after the officer driving it left the keys in the ignition while he stopped at a shopping center. Witnesses said that the two drove with the lights flashing and siren wailing, forcing other drivers to pull over, while they drank beer and threw the bottles on the backseat. Police finally caught the two when they stopped to buy more beer.

• Kansas City, Missouri, authorities charged Dale Richardson, twenty, with snatching a purse from a woman dining with a friend at a restaurant. The victim was the Jackson County prosecuting attorney Claire McCaskill. After making off with the purse, the suspect reportedly called McCaskill's house and offered to return the purse, which contained $50 cash and her prosecutor's badge, for a $250 reward. A police officer posing as McCaskill's baby-sitter, met the suspect, who was arrested soon after.

What It Means to Have a "Jones"

Frenchman Philippe Delandtscheer, sixty, was arrested for the fifty-first time for stealing a bottle of a French anise-flavored aperitif—just two days after he had been let out of prison for the previous robbery.

Some Days You Just Can't Win

Police in London investigating the theft of a $1,560 cockatoo questioned Clive McLoud about his bird. McLoud said that his bird was named Billy. Skeptical about his claims, police took Billy to the pet shop where the theft had occurred. The cockatoo recog-

nized the pet shop owner, said hello, and told police
that its name was Primrose.

JUSTICE AT ANY COST
A jury in Leeds, England, acquitted a twelve-year police
veteran of charges that he stole a calculator worth
$2.37 from the police station. The officer said that he
merely borrowed the calculator to check the books of
the police soccer team. The trial was the second in the
case, the first having ended in a mistrial. The prosecu-
tion of both trials and the defendant's fourteen-month
paid suspension cost taxpayers a total of $158,000.

ALL RIGHT—UP TO A POINT
In St. Paul, Minnesota, two masked gunmen claiming to
be police officers burst into a home and tied up a thirty-
nine-year-old woman and her two teenagers with duct
tape. The men wore black pants and black T-shirts with
the word *Police* but had panty hose over their faces, according to the woman, who said they asked for a man
and, when told he didn't live there, said, "Damn, we got
the wrong house."

ONE MORE FOR THE ROAD

Police in Hemet, California, arrested a thirty-three-year-old man, charging him with public drunkenness and allowing a juvenile to drive his car. Too drunk to drive home, the man had told his twelve-year-old son to take the wheel of his pickup truck. Police said that when they began pursuit, the man told his son "not to stop, just slow down and drive home." Police chased the truck home at 15 mph.

OPPORTUNITY KNOCKS

In Texas two inmates in the Wise County Jail's work program drove off with the sheriff's 1995 Jeep Grand Cherokee while washing patrol cars. "They were moving the car and they just took off with it," said the chief deputy in the sheriff's office. "It's just sort of something that's indigenous to the job." Said the sheriff: "We were allowing them to go around the building, which is out of sight. I didn't think that was a good idea, but I paid the price for letting that thought linger."

TRAVEL HAZARD

Kentucky State Police trying to stop a driver accused of leaving a gas station without paying deployed the stinger, a sixteen-foot strip of 110 spikes designed to puncture tires. The fugitive missed the spikes, but eight passing cars ran over them, deflating twenty tires. One of the innocent motorists, Lewis Morris, said troopers motioned him to the left and over the spikes, explaining, "Like blind sheep, we were all led across this thing." Trooper Jan Wuchner blamed miscommunication between the officer in pursuit and the one setting out the spikes.

INJUDICIOUS JUDGES

• When New York City police approached a car where they had seen four men place two large duffel bags, the men fled. Police searched the trunk and found eighty pounds of cocaine. The driver confessed in a forty-minute videotaped statement that this was one of more than twenty large drug buys she had made in Manhattan. Judge Harold Baer threw out the confession, ruling it stemmed from an unreasonable search since the fact that the police observed four men running away was not unusual. He explained that since residents in the area regard the police as corrupt and abusive, what would have been unusual would have been if they had not fled.

• Maryland's Commission on Judicial Disabilities publicly scolded Judge Henry J. Monahan for failing to evacuate his court during a fire. Warren Oden, the first bailiff to announce the fire, testified that Monahan reprimanded him for approaching the bench in an unorthodox fashion, then dismissed his suggestion that the judge call a recess. Another bailiff, John Matthews, who interrupted the proceedings a minute later to urge an evacuation, said the judge sharply scolded him and said, "This is my courtroom, and I run it as I please. Do you understand me?" The commission ruled the judge should behave more humbly and that his judgment "should not be clouded by his belief in his own stature, importance or significance (real or perceived)."

• Ohio Judge Albert Mestemaker sentenced a man accused of domestic violence to marry his alleged victim. "I believe the bonds of marriage might make an abuser think a little bit more before resorting to physical force," said the judge. "I believe strongly in family values."

• In Cleveland, Common Pleas Judge Shirley Strickland Saffold told a nineteen-year-old woman who had pleaded guilty to misusing a credit card to dump her boyfriend and find a doctor. "All of the women in prisons across these United States of America are there because of a guy," she said, adding, "Men are easy. You can go sit in the bus stop, put on a short skirt, cross your legs and pick up twenty-five. Ten of them will give you their money. If you don't pick up the first ten, then all you got to do is open your legs a little bit and cross them at the bottom and then they'll stop."

• Brooklyn Judge David Friedman threw out evidence police collected against an accused rapist because the evidence was found at night. Friedman explained that the warrant permitted a search "any time of the day." He noted that "day" referred only to the hours between 6:00 A.M. and 9:00 P.M., as is specified in Criminal Procedure Law 690.

• A judge in New Hampshire ruled that the marijuana found during a search of a twenty-one-year-old college student's dorm room couldn't be used as evidence against him because the student was too stoned to give his legal consent to the search in the first place.

HAZARDS OF BEING WELL ORGANIZED

After Travis Crabtree, fifteen, was charged with murdering Seeta Haddadi during a holdup at a Dallas beauty salon, police said part of the evidence against him was a floor plan of the shop and step-by-step instructions for the robbery, including a reminder to himself to kill his victim.

IN DENIAL

When police responded to a bank alarm in Columbus, Ohio, they caught Timothy E. Lebo, thirty-nine, and Charles J. Kinser, thirty-two, in a bank parking lot with a battered automated teller machine chained to their car. The men were arrested even though they insisted it wasn't an ATM but a washing machine.

REAL OR MEMOREX?

Motorcyclist Michael Cringle, thirty-three, was arrested in Eureka, California, after he gave police officer Matt Duran the finger, then led him on a chase that reached speeds of 120 mph. Cringle explained he thought Duran was a police department mannequin that occasionally is propped up in a patrol car to trick drivers into slowing down. "He flipped off the wrong dummy," Duran said.

TATTLETALE

• Three months after his indictment on charges stemming from having sex with a fifteen-year-old girl, Edward L. Jeffords, twenty-one, of Perryville, Maryland, appeared with three of his friends on the *Jerry Springer Show* to tout the advantages of having sex with minors. "You must have rocks in your head," Cecil County Circuit Judge Dexter M. Thompson, Jr., told Jeffords just before sentencing him to five years in prison. "Not only do you do this, do the offense, get indicted, and then you go on the show and talk about it."

• When customs agents at New York's Kennedy Airport charged Colombian native Carlos Trujillo, thirty, with not reporting currency of more than $10,000 after they found $60,100 hidden in a knapsack on a Mickey Mouse doll in his luggage and $10,495 in his pockets, Trujillo volunteered that he had another $18,900 in

$100 bills rolled up in twenty-seven condoms that he had swallowed.

WHY THEY CALL IT DOPE

• New Jersey trooper Glenn Lubertazzi stopped a car for speeding and was questioning the three occupants when one of them, Tina Stigger, thirty, asked if she could have a cigarette from a pack in the car's glove compartment. While handing the pack to the woman, he noticed it contained a marijuana joint. Authorities reported that a search of the vehicle turned up thirty-two thousand dollars in suspected drug buy money, marijuana, and drug paraphernalia.

• Law enforcement officials in Washington, D.C., discovered more than two hundred marijuana plants growing throughout a house during a search and arrested homeowner James Rapp and a tenant, Barry Oliver, forty-four. U.S. Secret Service spokesperson David M. Adams explained that the only reason authorities searched the house was that they had traced a call by one of the men threatening the president. According to WRC-TV, Oliver was tape-recorded saying that he had "a score to settle with President Clinton" and planned to "cut him from ear to ear."

CABBAGE PATCH DISPATCH

In Pittsburgh a jury ruled that the Pennsylvania Department of Transportation was not liable for the car accident that Sarah Milliken, forty-eight, claimed caused her to lose a year's wages after she suffered a broken back. A highlight of the evidence that Deputy Attorney General Robert McDermott used to prove Milliken was able to perform strenuous activity was a videotape provided by her estranged husband showing her and another woman in bathing suits wrestling in coleslaw during Bike Week activities in Daytona Beach, Florida, a year after the incident.

TITHES THAT BIND

Linda Siefer, the former church secretary at St. Michael's Roman Catholic Church in Kalida, Ohio, was convicted of stealing more than $411,000 in cash over a four-year period, taking all the $20 bills from collection plates. The theft was discovered when bank employees wondered why there were never any $20 bills in the church's deposits. "If she hadn't gotten greedy," prosecutor Dan Gerschutz said, "we might not have caught her."

ROBBERY, ITALIAN-STYLE

Sergio Magnis, Ferdinando Attanasio, and Antonio La Marra robbed at least five banks in two months in broad daylight and wearing no masks. After each robbery police arrested the men but had to release them under a 1993 Italian law that prohibits the jailing of people known to have the AIDS virus. At a press conference the men recalled they met one another outside an AIDS treatment center and were discussing their hardships until Magnis said, "I know where the money is." Although the men said they robbed banks only to draw attention to "our sickness," Turin's police chief, Giuseppe Grassi, called the gang "three criminals who have lost any sense of shame."

POOR TIMING

El Paso County, Colorado, sheriff's deputies arrested Edward Neidrick, thirty-four, on suspicion of driving under the influence after his car plowed into a sheriff's office DUI patrol van containing two other drunken-driving suspects.

ALL IN THE FAMILY

A Hawaiian appeals court overturned the conviction of James G. Kahoonei, declaring that his bedroom had been searched illegally. Kahoonei's mother had conducted the search, but the intermediate court of appeals decided that she wasn't acting as a mother when she looked for weapons but as an agent of the government.

MONEY MATTERS

In Dothan, Alabama, U.S. District Judge Myron Thompson granted two million dollars in legal fees to the nineteen lawyers it took to win a one-dollar judgment on behalf of consumers in a gasoline price-fixing case.

CAPTIVE AUDIENCES

• Twenty-five prisoners were having a barbecue in the prison yard at Denmark's Vridsloeslille State Jail, watched by only two guards, when a bulldozer smashed through the wall. Twelve of the men, identified as Denmark's most dangerous convicts, rushed through the opening. Almost a month later one of them, Kim Steven Kyed, twenty-seven, showed up at the main gate at 2:00 A.M., begging guards to let him back in. Police inspector Kai Hermann explained that Kyed was "homesick" for jail comforts.

• Keith Young, an inmate at the Greenville, Mississippi, jail, slipped out a door open to kitchen workers so he could visit his girlfriend. He stuffed the lock with paper to keep the door from latching behind him. Deputies found the paper, however, and removed it. When Young returned the next morning, he couldn't get in and returned to his girlfriend's. That night he telephoned deputies to come get him. "I've locked many a one up," Sheriff Harvey Tackett said, "but this is the first time I ever locked one out."

• Elsewhere in Mississippi, two inmates at the Perry County Jail escaped after discovering that the new rear door had been installed upside down, preventing the lock from working. Sheriff Carlos Herring explained jailers hadn't realized the door was upside down because the lock had a metal block around it to keep people from jimmying it.

• Three inmates at the Lew Sterrett Center in downtown Dallas gouged a two-and-one-half foot hole in the wall of the building from their fifth-floor cell. They tied together torn bedsheets and were climbing down the wall to a courtyard, according to Dallas County sheriff's department spokesperson Jim Ewell, when a cellmate they left behind apparently cut the bedsheet loose. One man plunged sixty-five feet to the ground and broke his back. The other two fell shorter distances but were unable to climb over the jail's fifteen-foot perimeter wall topped with razor wire. A woman arriving to post bail for another prisoner discovered the three convicts huddled in the courtyard in the twenty-degree weather yelling for help.

• George Delvecchio, forty-seven, a convicted murderer on death row in Illinois, asked for a stay of execution because a recent heart attack had left him too ill to be killed. Delvecchio said that his medication and his level of incoherence made him unfit for execution.

• Six inmates successfully escaped from a maximum security prison in Pittsburgh using a jackhammer and other power tools that authorities had provided inmates working on a steam-fitting project. The inmates also used blueprints of the project to guide their escape.

BALL AND CHAIN

Instead of returning Tonya Kline, a rebellious fifteen-year-old with a history of delinquency, to a Columbia, South Carolina, detention center until her sentencing on charges of truancy, shoplifting, and breaking into a house, Family Court Judge Wayne Creech on December 7 ordered her chained to her mother, Deborah Harter, twenty-four hours a day. Tonya was instructed to wear a traditional prisoner's belt with wrist and ankle shackles. Harter was told to hold a metal ring attached to the belt by a short chain and to accompany her daughter everywhere except the bathroom.

A week after the two were tethered, Harter complained to reporters that she and her husband, Richard, weren't able to spend any time alone together or go out with friends. "This is a very stressful situation the judge has put me in," she said. "I feel like I've got a sentence here as well."

On December 18 the judge said the mother and daughter could switch from the leather belt and metal shackles to a nylon belt with a strap and that Harter could share responsibility for holding on to Tonya with her husband.

On December 20 Harter acknowledged that she was being charged with contempt of court after being accused of letting go of the tether and smoking a cigarette while accompanying her daughter to school. Harter denied the allegations but admitted, "I'm having a hard time getting adjusted to this."

On January 9 Harter was rushed to the hospital for overdosing on a prescription drug for anxiety. Her husband assumed responsibility for holding his stepdaughter's leash.

On February 8 Richard Harter had to return to his job, so the judge asked the state to arrange for a hired helper to hold Tonya's leash. He order the mother to pay twenty-five dollars a month for the service.

Finally, on February 13, Creech ordered Tonya placed in state custody, saying her home was no place for her to be and that to return her there "is an invitation to disaster."

NICE TRY

Erwin Davis appealed his child support order to the Arkansas Supreme Court, claiming his DNA matched the child's only because the mother broke into his home, stole a used condom from him, and inseminated herself. Unimpressed, the court upheld the order.

WHAT'S THE BIG IDEA?

After his slimming salon, Inches Be Gone, went out of business, 485-pound Arthur Younkin was convicted of forging checks. He told Sedgwick County, Kansas, District Judge Clark Owens he couldn't afford to pay $11,333 in restitution because his weight kept him from working. The judge ordered Younkin to follow a strict diet, lose weight, and maintain the loss. After four months at a work release center Younkin lost 70 pounds and convinced the judge to let him live on his own. Younkin immediately gained 78 pounds and was hauled back into court. He confessed he was unable to resist nondiet soda and cream-filled cookies. By the time the judge sentenced Younkin to three months in jail for violating probation, his weight was up to 505 pounds.

WRONG PLACE, WRONG TIME

• Three men in a stolen car trying to elude police in Alexandria, Virginia, decided to ditch the car. They stopped on the shoulder of an expressway and ran north—directly toward Alexandria police headquarters. When pursuing officers sounded the alert, K-9 officers and their dogs were outside conducting a training session. In addition, the department was changing shifts, so there were nearly twice as many officers around headquarters as usual. At least twenty officers and several K-9 dogs gave chase, quickly arresting the suspects, according to police lieutenant John Crawford, who noted, "So many units responded to the call, it would be hard to credit each unit."

• When police at the Criminal Justice Center in Memphis, Tennessee, got a call that someone had robbed a bank three blocks away, officers looking out a twelfth-floor window could see the suspect running straight for the towering brick building, which houses the city police department, the Shelby County sheriff's department, and the county's criminal courts and is next door to the jail. As they directed officers on the ground, police in the building watched the suspect duck behind a law office, stash the dye-stained cash behind an air conditioner, then hustle up the walkway to the center. After pulling on locked glass doors, the suspect turned and faced a group of officers with guns drawn. Inspector Joe Holt reported the suspect "was overheard to make a statement to the effect, 'This isn't the police department, is it?' "

FORMS OVER FUNCTION

The Florida Supreme Court twice overturned death sentences of convicted killers because Circuit Court Judge Jay B. Rosman failed to complete the necessary paperwork justifying the sentences. Calling Rosman's oversight "more than a mere technicality," the justices ordered one of the men to be resentenced to a life term and the other released, even though Justice Charles

Wells said the idea of such a murderer going free because of a procedural oversight was "abhorrent."

DON'T LOOK NOW

The attorney for Howard ("Wing Ding") Jones, accused of selling drugs, sought to lower his client's bail from $150,000, insisting in a Norristown, Pennsylvania, courtroom that Jones was not a risk to flee. At that very moment Jones bolted from the courtroom and sprinted out the front door. Police captured him fifty minutes later and returned him to the courtroom, where his bail was promptly raised to $500,000.

GET-POOR-QUICK SCHEMES

• After Pelham, New Hampshire, house painter Phillip W. Cappella, thirty-four, won a $2.7-million lottery jackpot that paid him $135,000 a year, he filed a tax return listing $135,716 in winnings and claiming a $65,000 deduction for gambling losses, saving himself about $20,150 in federal taxes. When he was audited, he produced 200,000 losing scratch-off tickets to back up his claim. Federal prosecutors said that rather than buying and scratching off 550 tickets every day for a year, Cappella actually rented them for $500 from a man who collected them from various sources, including the trash. "The one consistent theme in virtually all white-collar criminal cases is greed," said Mark Pearlstein, chief of the U.S. Attorney's Office Economic Crimes Unit, "and it's my view that this case is well within that theme."

• FBI agents in Jacksonville, Florida, arrested brothers Robert Alberton, fifty-four, and Kenneth Alberton, forty-nine, accusing them of talking dentist John Rende into letting them chop off his finger with an ax so they could claim it was an accident and collect a fortune in insurance money. Rende at first agreed to the scheme, then changed his mind. The Albertons forcibly cut off his right index finger anyway. Unable to continue practicing dentistry, Rende collected $1.3 million. He paid the brothers $45,000. Later they tried to extort $500,000, so he notified the FBI.

Two's a Crowd

Prosecutors in Prince William County, Virginia, dropped rape and sodomy charges against a forty-five-year-old man who told police that one of the victim's multiple personalities had consented to have sex with one of his own multiple personalities. Citing insufficient evidence, prosecutor James T. Willet said the man explained that since he met the woman in group therapy, many of their different selves have fallen in love and even talked of marriage.

THINGS DON'T ADD UP

A Swedish court convicted a thirty-four-year-old taxi
driver of overcharging a forty-nine-year-old woman after he left the meter running while he had sex with her.
According to the *Aftonbladet* newspaper, the driver
billed the woman the equivalent of eighty-three hundred dollars for twenty-five occasions of "sexual services." The bill included twenty-five percent sales tax,
plus charges for trips, hotel, and telephone calls. A district court ruled the driver had exploited the woman's
longing for physical love.

LOOK BEFORE YOU LEAP

• A burglar who broke into a house in Wheatley
Heights, New York, beat up homeowner Conrad
Schwarzkopf, ninety-two, and shoved him in a closet.
The closet was where Schwarzkopf kept his pistol. He
opened the closet door and shot the burglar, who fled
but was arrested shortly after.

• In Coral Springs, Florida, Carl Lee Reese, twenty-
one, forced the driver of a Lexus into the trunk. As he
drove off, with an accomplice following in a station
wagon, the carjacker worried that the owner had a cellular phone in his pocket. Victim Paul Brite, fifty-three,
didn't have a phone, but he did keep two pistols in the
trunk. According to police, when Reese opened the
trunk, Brite shot him dead.

• Police in Bari, Italy, arrested a man suspected of snatching handbags to finance his drug addiction after he sped past a woman on his motorcycle and snatched her purse. The woman happened to be his mother, who recognized him and reported him.

She's a People Person

Shortly after winning New York State's Mrs. Congeniality contest, Barbara Ricci of Mount Vernon was retried on charges that she attempted to run down the eleven-year-old daughter of a neighbor with whom she was feuding. The first trial ended with a hung jury, but this time Ricci was acquitted. Asked what made the difference, David Hebert of the Westchester County district attorney's office pointed out "she took the stand in the first trial."

Reasonable Explanation

In Sonora, California, Gary Gunderson, forty-three, was convicted of grand theft and embezzlement after officials testified he had stolen truckloads of government property, ranging from tent straps and ready-to-eat meals to furniture and a five-thousand-watt generator. At his sentencing hearing, the former Forest Service worker explained to Judge William Polley that he didn't realize how much he had stolen because his eyesight was so poor he couldn't see it.

HIT-AND-MISS PROPOSITION

A federal trial in Philadelphia that resulted in the conviction of mob boss John Stanfa featured testimony by his inept hit men: Philip Colletti, John Veasey, and Rosario Conti Bellocchi. Veasey described using a power drill to torture a man but explained, "The drill bit broke."

He and Colletti said they were driving down a street in August 1993 when they spotted Stanfa's rival, Joseph ("Skinny Joey") Merlino, and opened fire. Although they killed his companion, they only wounded Merlino, then realized their car could be traced to Colletti since it was leased in his name. They planned to report it stolen, but first they doused it with gasoline. Just as Colletti tossed a match, Veasey spotted some coins inside and reached for them. At home he had to soak his severely burned hand in lighter fluid and set it on fire a second time to establish an alibi, informing neighbors who heard his very real screams that he had burned himself trying to light a grill.

Bellocchi told how he ran into a restaurant and leveled a shotgun at the pizza maker, an out-of-favor gang member. "I put the shotgun in his face and I shoot," Bellocchi testified. "The shotgun didn't go off. I shoot again. Again nothing." Finally he discovered he had loaded the weapon with the wrong-size shells.

REACH OUT AND TOUCH SOMEONE

• Police in Fort Smith, Arkansas, arrested Gary Wayne French, thirty-three, on felony drug charges after he mistakenly dialed the home phone number of Officer James Hammond and left a message on Hammond's answering machine. "Hey, I've got your dope and the money over here. Call me," he said, and gave a phone number that led officers to him.

• Police in Ogden, Utah, looking for the suspect who stole a pager, along with other items from two cars, activated the pager's number. An hour later their page was answered, and they traced the call to a motel room, where officers arrested a thirteen-year-old boy.

CURSES, FOILED AGAIN

• Police investigating a burglary in suburban Miami arrested Rafael Santiago, thirty-four, after they found his missing thumb at the scene of the crime. Metro-Dade police said Santiago shot his thumb off while he and an accomplice were trying to steal a shotgun from the apartment. The suspects fled, but Santiago was nabbed when he showed up at Jackson Memorial Hospital for treatment of his wound.

• Antonino Votano, an Italian gangster who was sentenced to life after a murder conviction but escaped, was apprehended after a year in hiding because he was a chain-smoker. Police spotted hundreds of fresh cigarette butts they recognized as Votano's brand outside a building that turned out to be his hideout, so they surrounded it and captured Votano without incident.

• When Peter Laurence Axelrod, forty-nine, robbed a bank in Oakland Mills, Maryland, he made certain to look directly at the bank's video camera, placed his hands on the counter to leave his fingerprints, and wrote in his holdup note that he would be waiting at his apartment. Quickly arrested, the fifty-eight-thousand-dollars-a-year personnel director at an industrial seal manufacturer in Baltimore explained he was tired of paying child support and figured he would be sent to a federal "country club" prison. He figured wrong. He was booked on state charges, which carry a maximum sentence of twenty-five years in a state penitentiary. Suddenly Axelrod was eager to beat the charge, and his lawyer argued that prosecutors had failed to prove his actions constituted a bank robbery.

• Los Angeles police arrested Michael Johnson, thirty-eight, on suspicion of trying to collect four hundred dollars by passing off 3,804 pennies as dimes. He reportedly put the pennies in dime rolls and presented them to a bank teller. But the mass of coin bundles and a wanted poster identifying Johnson as a suspect in two similar incidents alerted bank officials, who checked the rolls and called police. Without an automatic coin counter, officers spent five and a half hours counting pennies to build their case against Johnson.

• Police in West Lafayette, Indiana, arrested Jeffrey J. Pyrcicoch and Heather M. Green, both nineteen, for passing checks filled out with purple disappearing ink. Even though five merchants who were victimized found the bogus checks blank when they went to cash them, police had no trouble tracking down the suspects because the checks had Pyrcicoch's name imprinted on them—in permanent ink.

• After Philadelphia police received a report that Jeremiah Allen, twenty-nine, had kidnapped his exgirlfriend at gunpoint and driven her to his apartment, an officer called Allen and asked him to drop by the police station. The suspect not only complied but even brought the woman with him, as well as his gun. "You know the guy can't be a rocket scientist," one officer said after Allen was arrested, "if he brings a gun with him to a police station."

• Police searching for a bank robber in Fairfax County, Virginia, had no trouble finding their suspect. They went into a nearby subway station and saw a man matching the robber's description standing on the platform and money covered with exploded dye hanging out of his pockets.

• Police in Cadiz, Kentucky, charged Kevin Stanley Stokes, twenty-five, with robbing a grocery store. After taking $170 at gunpoint, the robber dashed out to his waiting getaway car to find the door locked and the keys inside. He had to kick out a back window to get into the car, giving police more than enough time to respond to the emergency call by store clerks.

• Police in Lexington, North Carolina, arrested three men for robbing a gas station after their getaway car swerved off the road and flipped over when the driver tried to steer and count the stolen money at the same time.

• Police in Highland, Indiana, arrested Mark Petraitis, twenty-four, for robbing a convenience store after the clerk identified him, even though he was wearing maroon underpants over his head. "He was wearing them sideways, using one of the leg holes to look through to hide his identity," police lieutenant Paul Gard said. "That didn't work so well because the clerk recognized him immediately because he had been in there often."

• Police in Golden, Colorado, arrested James Daly, twenty-eight, after they reported he was confronted during a burglary by the homeowners. He fled, scaled a fence, tumbled down a hill, fell under the wheel of a moving car, and crashed into a bicycle ridden by a police officer. The suspect resumed running, but officers spotted him trying to hide behind a bush that they said offered very little cover.

• Colorado Springs, Colorado, police lieutenant Steve Liebowitz was driving an unmarked car with two sergeants when he spotted a car going 50 mph and started to follow it. A white Regency got between the cars, Liebowitz said, "then made an unsafe lane change, cut me off and proceeded past the vehicle we were clocking." Liebowitz pulled the Regency over and asked for identification. Explaining he had no license because it had been revoked, the driver offered as identification a newspaper clipping with a photo proving he was Brandon Clary, twenty. The story told that Clary was standing trial on charges of causing a fatal traffic accident. Leibowitz ticketed Clary for unsafe driving.

• Thomas Springer, forty-six, pleaded guilty to robbing a bank in Fairfax County, Virginia, after he was caught while making his getaway because he stopped to urinate in bushes and was spotted. Springer, a former aide to four members of Congress, told the court he committed the crime after he lost his latest job when his boss, Representative Michael Forbes, R-New York, learned of Springer's previous conviction for bank robbery, which also occurred after he lost a congressional job.

• Police in Takoma Park, Maryland, charged Gary Jay Coates, twenty-six, with robbing a woman at an automated teller machine. As the suspect sprinted away from the ATM, his baggy pants dropped to his knees. The man pulled up his pants and continued running, but by this time police had caught up with him.

• Miami police arrested three suspects in the robbery of a grocery store after they pulled their guns and two of them shot each other. Witnesses said the three gunmen ordered the clerks to the floor and demanded that the cash register be opened. Jeanis Caty, eighteen, started to reach over the counter to grab the money but accidentally fired his gun, striking Wesley Steny, sixteen, in the thigh. Surprised and in pain, Steny tripped over clerk Mariano Gonzalez, causing him to fire off a round that hit Caty in the leg. "I've had robbers shoot themselves before," Detective Tom Pellechio of Miami's Metro-Dade police said, "but I never had two robbers shoot each other."

• Sheriff's deputies searching a burglarized house outside Sacramento, California, found the suspect, Brett Woolley, twenty-five, inside asleep in the bathtub while taking a bubble bath.

• As Sacramento police officers were questioning the witness to a stabbing death, Philip Lenford Allen, forty, strolled past leading a pit bull on a leash. "The witness tells us, 'Hey, there he is right there,'" Sergeant John Parker said, noting that the dog was the same one the suspect had had with him when he fought with the victim. After a search of Allen's home turned up blood-stained clothes and a knife, Parker explained the suspect apparently changed clothes and "came back figuring that nobody could identify him."

• A twenty-seven-year-old Maryland woman was driving away from a gas station in Alexandria, Virginia, when she discovered a man hiding in the backseat of her car. He told her to find a secluded area where they could have sex. According to Fairfax County police, the woman noticed a house with its lights on and told her abductor it was her uncle's home and they could use a room there. The man let the victim go to the door alone. She explained the situation to the resident, whom she didn't know, then went inside and called police. They found Sylvester Moore, forty-three, still standing on the front porch waiting to be let into the house.

• After sneaking into a St. Louis health center and hiding in the bathroom until the building closed, Ronald Haegele, thirty-two, discovered the valuable medical equipment and medication he hoped to take had been locked up. He settled for stuffing his pockets with office supplies, then realized there was no way out. His solution to the predicament was to call 911 and explain he had gotten locked in the building after a guard had let him in to use the bathroom, then forgotten about him. When Officer Deborah Reinarman arrived to investigate the call, she recognized Haegele, whom she had previously arrested for burglary. She also noticed pens, pencils, and a stapler sticking out of his pockets and arrested him. "It was just nickel and dime stuff he could sell real fast for drugs," Reinarman said, adding, "He's not a very bright guy."

• Undeterred by the Closed for Private Party sign, Clarisse Wynn, twenty, and Darvie Sutton, forty-three, entered Z's Sports Tap bar in downtown Chicago. Finding more than a hundred partygoers inside, they lured owner Tammy Bertucci away from behind the bar, then brandished a knife and demanded money. Unimpressed, Bertucci called for help. Most of the revelers turned out to be police officers attending a colleague's retirement party. Several gave chase and quickly nabbed the suspects.

• Five gunmen entered the Provident Savings Bank in Jersey City, New Jersey, filled duffel bags with cash, and fled. Witnesses inside and outside the bank spotted the armed masked men piling into a gold Cadillac with New York plates. It didn't take police long to find the car and arrest the suspects. "It was a rather distinctive car," Assistant U.S. Attorney Amy Winkelman noted. "It was not exactly inconspicuous."

• In Arlington, Virginia, a man presented a check for $1,450 to a bank teller, who told him to wait for approval and took the check to the assistant vice-president Melinda Babson. She knew the woman whose check it was but didn't recognize the signature, so she called her. The woman said she had not written the check, which Babson then copied and faxed to her. The whole time the unsuspecting suspect waited calmly, sipping a cup of coffee, according to the senior vice-president Andrew Flott, who noted after police arrived and arrested the man, "he was a knucklehead for not leaving." Even if he had left, the teller had his driver's license, which he had given her for identification with the check.

• A man in Stockton, California, robbed a department store cashier and stole a tourist's car to make his getaway. Police had no trouble identifying Omhar Leyva, twenty-four, as their suspect because he appeared on a videotape by a local television cable company that was filming a commercial outside the store.

• In Mexico three armed state police officers surrounded a car containing the eldest son of President Ernesto Zedillo and, apparently unaware of their victim's identity, demanded money. They learned soon enough who he was when another car containing presidential bodyguards stopped, and the guards overpowered the police.

• After stealing money from coin-operated washing machines in an apartment building in Elizabeth, New Jersey, at 4:00 A.M., the thief tipped over the machines, breaking the water pipes connected to them and spraying water all over. The sound of the machines hitting the floor and the running water awoke the building superintendent, who spotted the thief running away and called police. Assistant Prosecutor Peter McCord told a grand jury that police spotted Robert Brown, thirty, moments later and arrested him because he was "dripping wet." He was also found to be carrying sixty-three quarters.

• In Chillicothe, Ohio, Vernon Viney, twenty-one, visited his ex-wife's house to videotape their child. According to police, he also unwittingly recorded himself slapping and threatening to kill the woman.

• Two escapees from a Utah state prison were arrested after being questioned by campus police at the University of California at Berkeley. Anthony Scott Bailey, twenty-seven, and Eric Neil Fischbeck, twenty-one, aroused suspicion by saying they were from "Frisco," a nickname for San Francisco that tourists use but residents disdain. When upon further questioning one provided two different spellings for his purported last name, officers took them in and discovered they were fugitives. Noting they were just four months away from parole but now faced up to fifteen more years for the escape, Utah corrections spokesperson Jack Ford said, "Anybody who escapes with that little time left can't be very smart."

• In the trial of six men charged with attempting Britain's biggest cash robbery, prosecuting lawyer Guy Boney told the court that the gang forced an armored car carrying $18.2 million to be driven to a wooded area, then used high-powered torches to open it. But, Boney noted, the torches also set off "a horrendously expensive bonfire" that turned up to $2.4 million into ashes and caused the men to flee.

• Police in Wloclawek, Poland, reported that four men went fishing with a high-voltage line attached to a net, designed to stun and capture the fish. For a while everything went according to the poachers' plan. Then a twenty-four-year-old man holding the net tripped and fell into the water, electrocuting himself.

• An armed man wearing a Halloween mask tried to rob the Cedar Glen Golf Course clubhouse in Saugus, Massachusetts, but fled after one patron pulled off his mask and the others laughed at him.

• A thirty-six-year-old man accused of stealing a hundred dollars' worth of film from a Baltimore drugstore was fleeing when he ran into a streetful of people in police uniforms. After surrendering to them, he learned they were actors dressed as police officers filming the NBC-TV show *Homicide* on location. The actors handed the suspect over to the store's security guard. "The judge should dismiss the charges," actor Richard Belzer said, "because he was punished with humiliation."

So Sue Me

• Two New York schoolgirls sued each other over which one of them deserved to be called the best. Lisa

Camilleri, eighteen, insisted she was told in the fall that she was to be her high school graduating class's valedictorian for having scored the highest grade point average over the previous six years. The following term, however, classmate Paige Goodman surpassed Camilleri's average, and she was named valedictorian. Camilleri's parents protested, so principal Harris Sarney declared that the two students would share the honor, prompting the Goodmans to sue. The New York Supreme Court heard the case and found for Goodman but then the following day restored the principal's ruling.

• A Littleton, Colorado, man sued Starbucks Corporation claiming that he was disabled for seven months after getting a high-five greeting from an ex-employee of one of the company's coffee shops.

• The Supreme Court refused to allow Bobbie June Griggs to sue a South Carolina utility that sponsored the publication of a cookbook, even though Griggs insisted that the publication of her recipe for a rice dish in the book without her permission caused her to have a nervous breakdown.

• John Leonard, a twenty-one-year-old business student, sued Pepsi for failing to fulfill its obligation in the 1995 ad campaign "Drink Pepsi, Get Stuff," which stated that consumers who collected points from Pepsi cans and bottles could turn them in to purchase "Pepsi Stuff" items. One item was a Harrier jet for seven hundred million merchandise points, which, at ten cents a point, equals $70 million. A test ad that ran in the Northwest, however, offered the jet for only seven million points. Since that would amount to 16.8 million Pepsis, Leonard called the company and said that he was told he had an option of buying "points" for ten cents each.

Leonard assembled five investors, sent Pepsi some points and a check for $700,008.50, and demanded his jet. Dismissing the claim as frivolous, the soft-drink company returned Leonard's check, pointing out that the Harrier offer wasn't real. Undaunted, Leonard hired an attorney to press his claim. "It was a joke," a Pepsi spokesperson said, "an outlandishly funny joke that all of America got, except for one guy, who, instead of laughing, gets a lawyer."

• After Cyril Smith, fifty-nine, was told by a hospital in Portsmouth, England, that he had lung cancer and only three months to live, he began chemotherapy treatment. Three years later he was still alive. The cancer had vanished. As a result, Smith announced he was suing the National Health Service for mental anguish and loss of wages from the job he quit because the agency said he would die, but he didn't. Then his cancer returned, for which he blamed chemotherapy.

• After being robbed at gunpoint in a Disneyland parking lot, former Mousketeer Billie Jean Matay filed a suit in Orange County, California, claiming she and her grandchildren suffered from negligence and emotional distress inflicted on them by security guards. Worst of all, the suit charges, during the hours of questioning they were subjected to after the incident, they caught glimpses of Disney characters taking off their costumes, "exposing the children to the reality that the Disney characters were, in fact, make-believe."

• In Norfolk, Virginia, Thomas Passmore, thirty-two, who cut off his right hand, then refused to let surgeons reattach it, filed a suit against the hospital and the doctors, seeking $3.35 million. He said the doctors at Sentara Norfolk General Hospital should have contacted his family to overrule his decision.

• Kevin Jalbert of Milford, Connecticut, filed a lawsuit against Phil Donahue and Marlo Thomas, seeking fifteen thousand dollars to cover medical bills and repairs to his pickup truck stemming from a 1994 accident when he turned to look at the couple's dog and drove into the back of a fire truck. His suit claimed the celebrity couple were negligent in allowing their five-year-old golden retriever to wander away from their Westport home and onto Interstate 95 a quarter mile away.

• An Israeli woman in Haifa filed a lawsuit in small claims court against popular television weatherman Danny Rup, seeking a thousand dollars after he predicted sun for a day that turned out stormy. The daily newspaper *Maariv* reported the woman claimed that because of Rup's forecast, she left home lightly dressed. As a result, she caught the flu, missed four days' work, and spent $38 on medication.

• Robert Lee Brock, serving twenty-three years at the Indian Creek Correctional Center in Chesapeake, Virginia, for breaking and entering and grand larceny, admitted it was his own fault that he got drunk and committed a series of crimes, so he sued himself for five million dollars for violating his own religious beliefs against drinking. Since he can't work and is a ward of the state, he said the state should pay the five million. Conceding Brock had "presented an innovative approach to civil rights litigation," Judge Rebecca Beach Smith nonetheless dismissed his claim as "ludicrous."

• Unable to stop Ku Klux Klansmen from their ritual cross burnings because the practice occurred on private property and is protected by the First Amendment, officials in Modesto, California, devised a new tactic. They announced they would file a civil suit against Bill Albers, who identifies himself as the Imperial Wizard of the California Klan, for violating air quality regulations by burning a thirty-foot gasoline-drenched cross. "I could care less what his politics are," said Philip Jay, attorney for the San Joaquin Valley Air Pollution Control District. "But when he's burning some burlap-wrapped, diesel-soaked cross made out of railroad ties, it's a pretty [clear] violation."

• Described by her lawyer as a "full-figured" model, not a "skinny" one, Laura Valentine, thirty-six, filed a $1.5 million lawsuit against a shopping mall in Dale City, Virginia, after a platform she was modeling clothes on collapsed beneath her weight. Attorney Thomas P. Maims, Jr., noted that since the incident his client has been "having trouble walking gracefully and elegantly."

• In Brazil retired beer taster Bernd Naveke sued the brewery he worked for, claiming it had turned him into an alcoholic. Seeking $160,000 in compensation, Naveke said he had drunk the equivalent of fifty thousand bottles of beer during his twenty years with the firm. A company official denied the charge, explaining that beer tasters need drink only a small amount of each sample, although they aren't prevented from drinking more.

TOO MUCH TIME ON THEIR HANDS

According to the National Association of Attorneys General, prisoner lawsuits take up about twenty percent of the federal docket. In 1994 more than thirty-nine thousand federal cases were filed by prisoners. They include:

• A convicted rapist who claimed "hardship" because he had been served a soggy sandwich and a broken cookie

• An Ohio inmate who said that his constitutional rights were being violated because he was not allowed to wear sunglasses

• A Florida prisoner who filed more that four hundred lawsuits, including one over having to eat off paper plates and another about being served a piece of cake that he claimed was not big enough

• Another Florida inmate who filed suit after lightning hit the prisoner's satellite dish, forcing him to watch network programming, which he found to contain violence and profanity

• A Michigan inmate who sued because his sweepstakes clearinghouse entry was not provided to him in time, charging that if it had been, he could have won the jackpot

• An Oregon inmate who claimed that prison officials refused to do anything about a regular early-morning train whistle that disturbed his sleep

SOURCES

Associated Press
Atlanta Constitution
Boston Globe
Boston Herald
Buffalo News
Charlotte Observer
Chicago Tribune
Chicago Sun-Times
Columbia Journalism Review
Columbus Dispatch (Ohio)
Commercial Appeal (Memphis, Tennessee)
Dallas Morning News
Denver Post
Des Moines Register
Detroit Free Press
Detroit News
Deutsche Presse-Agentur

The European
Fortean Times
Globe and Mail
Harper's
Herald Times (Bloomington, Indiana)
International Herald Tribune
Kansas City Star
Knoxville News-Sentinel (Tennessee)
Los Angeles Times
Miami Herald
Minneapolis Star Tribune
Naples Daily News (Florida)
Nashville Banner (Tennessee)
New Scientist
New York Daily News
New York Newsday
New York Post
New York Times
Newsweek
Parade
People
Philadelphia Daily News
Philadelphia Inquirer
Plain Dealer (Cleveland)
Post-Standard (Syracuse, New York)
Reuters
Rocky Mountain News
Roll Call
St. Louis Post-Dispatch
San Francisco Chronicle
San Jose Mercury News (California)
Seattle Times
Star-Ledger (Newark, New Jersey)
Syracuse Herald-Journal (New York)

Sun (Baltimore)
Sun-Sentinel (Fort Lauderdale, Florida)
Tampa Tribune
Tennessean (Nashville)
Texas Monthly
Times-Picayune (New Orleans)
Time
United Press International
USA Today
U.S. News & World Report
Wall Street Journal
Washington Post
Washington Times
World Press Review